Prais

Christine takes you, the reader, on a wonderful journey in Project: LIFE. Her own story is shared with warmth and vulnerability, honesty and humility, and this is only half the story. The other half is about you the reader, and Christine offers the tools and techniques for you to create the LIFE you were born to live! A must-read for every woman!

—Dr Peta Stapleton,
Clinical & Health Psychologist,
Associate Professor School of Psychology Bond University,
and author of *The Science Behind Tapping*

Christine's journey is deep. She's a warrior committed to sharing the practical steps we can all use to transcend our circumstances, past or present, regardless of what they may be, and cultivate our true and unconditional happiness.

—Kary Oberbrunner,
author of *Day Job to Dream Job*

Not only for women! This book is also for men who are open to changing their lives and seeing the world differently or who have simply reached the end and need a life line. In Project: LIFE, Christine shares her story in a relatable way that truly touches your mind, body, and soul. Not only that, but she shares the core tools she applied in her life that will inspire and equip you to create change. Project: LIFE is about healing, feeling, awakening, and spiritual growth. It proves that you can make your own happiness happen!

—Darcy Patrick,
author of *Why I Run*

To say that I was inspired by this book is an understatement! I LOVED it! I've read it twice. It shows that whatever happens to us doesn't define us. It can make us stronger if we choose to love life. Sometimes the past creeps in and brings me down, but now I have some tools to help me get back on track quickly. I really found the second half of the book to be invaluable—I've read that part three times! Love shines through this book—reading it has been a gift for which I am so grateful.

—Marcie Fry,
life learner

A must-read! Incredibly moving and life-changing for every soul! Christine shares her life story along with the practical and proven tools she incorporates daily to manifest unconditional happiness and love!

—Cheryl Thomas,
mother and life learner

Project: LIFE

Stop Waiting for Your Happy to Happen

Project: LIFE

Stop Waiting for Your Happy to Happen

CHRISTINE GRAUER, M.Sc.

Printed in the United States of America.

Published by Author Academy Elite
PO Box 43, Powell, OH 43035
www.AuthorAcademyElite.com

Available in paperback, hardcover, ebook, and audiobook

Library of Congress Control Number: 2020903535
ISBN: 978-1-64746-159-1 (paperback)
ISBN: 978-1-64746-160-7 (hardback)
ISBN: 978-1-64746-161-4 (ebook)

Any internet addresses (websites, blogs, etc.) printed in this book are offered as a resource. They are not intended in any way to be or imply an endorsement by Author Academy Elite, nor does Author Academy Elite vouch for the content of these sites for the life of this book.

Cover design by: 99Designs.com *(MeltProject)*
Interior design by: JetLaunch

Disclaimer

The suggestions in this book are the opinions and ideas of its author. This book is distributed with the understanding that the author and publisher are not engaged in rendering medical, health, or any other kind of personal or professional services in the book. The suggestions in this book are not a substitute for the medical advice of a physician or other healthcare professional. The reader should consult a physician in matters relating to their health before adopting the suggestions within this book or drawing inferences from it.

The author and publisher disclaim all responsibility for any liability, loss, or risk, personal or otherwise, that is incurred as a direct or indirect consequence of the use and application of any of the contents of this book.

Some names and identifying characteristics have been changed to protect the privacy of individuals.

Dedication

This book is dedicated to every woman whose turbulent past
has defined her in some limiting way
and buried the light and truth of who they are.

It's for the women who know that there's something more
going on in this project called LIFE
and that there has got to be another way.

It's for the women who are finally ready to make a change.

Stop waiting for your happy to happen—
it's time to create it.

Owning our story can be hard
but not nearly as difficult as spending our lives running from it.
Embracing our vulnerabilities is risky
but not nearly as dangerous as giving up on love
and belonging and joy—
the experiences that make us the most vulnerable.
Only when we are brave enough to explore the darkness
will we discover the infinite power of our light.

—Brené Brown

Contents

Contents

Note to Reader

Dear Friend,

Like most lives, mine has included several adventures, many of which were undesirable (to put it mildly). But everyone has a story, right?

So, why this story?

We've all had moments in our past that have left us feeling bad, sad, ashamed, guilty, wronged, or furious. And too often these feelings carry into our futures and impact our lives in devasting ways. I've seen the healing power that vulnerability and authenticity can bring to others, so I'm sharing my story in hopes of helping you realize that, despite where you've been, where you are today, and where you're heading tomorrow, you already possess the necessary tools to create change and live the life you desire.

The words within this book contain some raw personal details that I have shared with few people, if any. None of my life events were happenstance—there was a theme and purpose to them all, great and small—and they've led me to become who I am today. I'm sharing them with you to help you see that the past does not define who we are today, unless we allow it.

I've divided this book into two parts: *My Story* and *Your Story*.

My Story is just that—my life story up to today. It's written as I have experienced life and to the best of my recollection. Some names and identifiers have been intentionally changed to protect the privacy of individuals. As I retell the events of my life, I write notes to my back-then-self—the *aha* moments that I learned decades later that, darn it, would have been handy to have known when I needed them!

In Part 2—*Your Story,* you'll find the lessons, tools, and techniques of the LIFE Method™ that I learned and applied after I woke up to the real story going on in my life. The tools and practices are simple and accessible for you to apply in your daily life, if you so choose, to cultivate more resilience, energy, ease, and happiness.

Skip Part 1 if you wish to get straight to the goods and cultivate your happy today.

The practices of the LIFE Method™ that I've learned and developed through my spiritual development and professional training have allowed me to remain centered and calm and to greet each challenge with curiosity and anticipation. With unmovable faith, I investigate within. Each challenge becomes an opportunity for my growth and expansion. And as I do my inner work, my outside circumstances shift and transformation occurs. Through this process, I've cultivated resilience, an amazing amount of energy, and deep love and compassion for all beings, as well as a capacity to thrive and experience unconditional happiness, regardless of my external conditions.

I've had a deep desire to share my story through writing, and many have encouraged me to do so. I am deeply honoured to share this journey with you.

My intention through this book is to inspire you and provide you with proven and practical tools because, regardless of your past experiences and current conditions, you too can transcend your circumstances and experience the vast amount of energy and happiness available at your fingertips.

You see, I'm an average person, just like you. I'm a single mom with two kids, a job, a house, and a Chihuahua. I didn't retreat to India to master myself and my life, but I did endure a heck of a past and an intense amount of training and inner work to be able to share this LIFE Method™ with you.

My wish is for you to bypass the painful experiences that otherwise would be needed to nudge you forward and upward in your life. You don't need to learn the hard way.

Seriously!

You can experience an amazing life and live your eternal happy now!

Ultimately, I hope this book helps you realize that your life is *yours* to direct—you are the scriptwriter of your story, and the sooner you realize this and take ownership of it, the sooner you'll create your dream LIFE—it can start today!

With great love and hope,
Christine

PART 1

MY STORY:

INTERNAL MINING

CHAPTER 1

Burying the Truth: Inheriting the Dirt

Beliefs are thought patterns that have become quite permanent and are formed early in life. We seek confirmation in our everyday life that our thoughts, and ultimately core beliefs and schemas, make sense to us... but they can be changed.
— Dr Peta Stapleton, *The Science Behind Tapping*

There's little I recall as a lanky girl growing up in our two-bedroom apartment near Toronto. But then again, there are some things etched in my memory which are hard to forget, like the time I was startled awake in my bunk bed in the middle of the night. Unsure of what was happening, I strained to see, but the room was blackened with only a dim light streaming through the crack at the base of the door. I was startled again. The noise was like nothing I'd heard before—it was horrendous and piercing. With my heart palpitating through my chest, I quickly and firmly tucked my head under my covers and listened some more. Between the shrill crashes, I could hear Apu's Hungarian music echoing in the background. The fast, aggressive tempo was unique and unlike any of the music I'd listened to from *Sesame Street* or from Mom's eight-track tape of *Abba*. Apu didn't play his Hungarian music often—only on special occasions. And this night was apparently one of them.

The crashes subsided, and with quieted breath I strained to decipher what was happening behind the droning sounds of the music. I wiped the sweat from my forehead as my breathing resumed to normal inside the condensation-filled cocoon of covers. Within moments, sounds of shattered ceramic brushing across the floor filled the air. As the Hungarian music faded, I drifted back to sleep.

There was no talk in the morning of what happened during the night, but the lack of dishes in the cupboards and the grooves etched in the kitchen floor told a clear story.

Mom was solemn and quiet.

A Family in the Making

Born in May of 1946, near Stuttgart, Germany, my mom was the youngest of nine girls and one boy, as well as another three siblings who died in their infancy. Raised post-World War Two, Mom's upbringing was shrouded with scarcity and conformity, with little time for play because the family needed to work hard to make ends meet. Mom was often tethered to the railing at the front of the house by a rope around her waist. There, she was left alone sucking on a cheesecloth packed with seeds from poppy flowers while her mom worked in the distant gardens.

Mom finished school at the age of fourteen and started working full-time in a yarn factory from seven in the morning until five in the evening. After a few years, she transitioned into a job as a nanny for a family with two boys. She didn't like her life of scarcity in Germany—she had a plan to save money and move to a Land of Plenty, just as her older sister had done. And at eighteen, my determined mom did just that. With only a small bag of clothes and enough money for airfare, she took flight to Canada. She had no knowledge of English and no money in her pocket.

When she arrived in Toronto, Mom was greeted by her sister with whom she stayed so she could gain some traction beneath her feet in this foreign land. With Mom's kind heart, brilliant smile, and her love of children, it took her no time to find work as a live-in nanny. The family with three young children knew no German, so Mom's knowledge of English grew exponentially by the day.

Within a few months of settling into her new job, Mom's church friend introduced her to a tall, dark, and handsome man—my dad. He instantly took a liking to Mom with her thin frame, blonde hair, and warm smile.

Daddy was born in Yugoslavia in 1936. As a young teen, he and his sister, two brothers, and parents moved to Frankfurt, Germany where he lived until he emigrated to Canada as a young adult. Shortly after settling in Toronto, he began to work as a watch repairman; with passion, purpose, and precision, he'd mend and guide the intricate components of broken watches to bring them back to life. Like Mom, Daddy was gentle, caring, and loving. They were two kind and kindred souls and soon fell in love.

Within a few months of meeting, my mom and dad married. Mom got a new job at a truck trading company, and together my parents saved and bought a house. They soon welcomed my sister, Angelina, into the world, and I joined the family in July of 1971.

With two healthy, beautiful daughters, a loving and caring husband, and a small house in Toronto, Mom was living the perfect life of which she had always dreamed. But, before I turned one, the trajectory of all our lives changed dramatically.

Daddy was diagnosed with Multiple Sclerosis, a neuro-degenerative disease. His health quickly deteriorated to the point where he was no longer able to move his fingers to work with the miniscule watch parts. As Daddy's health and mobility continued to decline, my parents sold our home and moved into Wyndham Place—an apartment building where they worked as the superintendents. The apartment provided our family with a home without the financial burden of rent or mortgage.

With two small children and superintendent responsibilities, caring for Daddy was too much for Mom to handle. She struggled to provide proper care for Daddy and his rapidly declining health. They were relieved to learn of advanced and promising medical treatment for Multiple Sclerosis in Germany, and since Daddy's parents were available to care for him full-time, my parents considered moving back to Germany. But Mom didn't want to return to her former life of scarcity. She didn't want Angelina and me to grow up as she did. So, discussions took place and plans shifted for Daddy to travel to Germany alone.

But Daddy wouldn't leave us behind without knowing that my mom, my sister, and I had reliable support—he was concerned about Mom's ability to handle the superintendent responsibilities, especially since Mom's English skills were still developing. So, Daddy asked Les, a family friend, to help us out. Feeling a little more at ease about leaving us in the good hands of Les, Daddy finalized his plans to leave.

Before I turned two, Daddy moved back to his parents' place in Germany to get well. Saddened, but with high hopes of Daddy soon returning in good health, my mom, my sister, and I remained in our apartment with Les available to provide support when it was needed.

The next time I saw Daddy was at his funeral in Germany when I was nine years old. I have no conscious memories of my dad, but I do remember his funeral. It was a cold day, and I wore a light brown coat that flared at the bottom and was lined with sheepskin at the collar. I remember not crying—I intentionally tried to be funny to dismiss the graveness of the gathering. I remember looking at the flowers and massive, shiny slabs of marble that lay flat on the ground covering others who had passed before. I tried to get my mom to look at all the things outside and around her as well, instead of feeling the loss and grief inside of her. I didn't want Mom to be sad and cry. I didn't want to be sad and cry. So, I didn't. I pretended to be happy and tried to cheer up the sad people around me.

> *Note to Self:* OMG. Cry, Girl, cry! Let it flow!

Life in Apartment 204

Les was the handyman for Wyndham Place. He sanded and finished the parquet floors in the apartments and did odd jobs, like change light fixtures, repair broken locks, and fix leaky faucets.

Mom was happy to have the help of a handyman around the building, but her heart belonged with Daddy. And despite Mom having no desire to be with Les, within a year he pushed his way into our apartment and began living with us. He became "Apu," which means *dad* in Hungarian. Apu was born in Hungary in 1938. His head was bald and shiny, except for a horizontal strip of grey, coarse hair that wrapped around the back from ear to ear. He was short and stocky, and with a frequent grimace on his face, he reminded me of a bulldog. He smoked a pack-and-a-half of cigarettes daily and drank litres of coffee which my mom faithfully prepared for him just the way he liked it: saturated with steamed milk and sugar. He had thick, tough hands, which were as coarse as the sandpaper he used to sand floors.

I loved Apu. I often sat on his knee at the kitchen table and ate morsels from the slabs of smoked bacon he'd cut up for me. I snuggled contently beside him on the couch, where he'd often be found when he wasn't working, and together we watched nature shows on television. I'd dream of going to Africa to see the things we watched on the screen—a dream I'd fulfill later in life. We played a little game, where I'd tickle his moustache, and he'd startle me by snorting and snapping, trying to snatch my finger in his mouth. I'd jump from being startled and then giggle with glee. Our cockatiel, Conrad, also enjoyed couch time with Apu. Anytime Apu was on the couch watching television, Conrad would be found on his chest, twirling a toothpick, which he had grabbed from Apu's mouth.

Apu was a hard worker, and the pride he took in sanding floors was apparent through his well-known, flawless shiny floors. When I grew older, I'd come to be his floor sanding assistant.

When Apu got home from work, he'd take off his work shoes (black, flat Chinese slippers) and I'd give him a hug. He greeted me with an enthusiastic, "Hiya, Baby!" with accompanying scents of wood, cigarettes, and coffee. Traces of sawdust fell from his eyelashes and bald head, which I'd brush off before returning to play or watch *Sesame Street*.

Not only was Apu's floor sanding and handyman work spot-on, his classic Hungarian cabbage rolls, stuffed peppers, and Poor Man soup with homemade egg-noodles were mouth-wateringly delicious. Scents of appetizing cooking, blended with second-hand smoke, would waft from our apartment door. We were *those people* who stunk up the hallway. But, we always had an open door, and tenants would simply knock and enter our apartment without waiting for an invitation. Everyone who entered was greeted by Mom or Apu with a sample of the delicious dish that was on the burner or table.

We had a warm and welcoming home, and I think the combination of Apu's open and welcoming approach and

Mom's loving kindness drew people to our place and made them want to hang out in our home.

I always remember Mom as being gentle, soft-spoken and ever so patient—with everyone. As a small girl, I relished in her soothing demeanor. I felt so calmed, relaxed, and nurtured to simply sit quietly by her side as she lightly tickled my arm with soft, gentle, rhythmic strokes, for what felt like hours on end. Even when Mom spanked us with the wooden spoon, it was soft and light. When Angelina and I grew slightly older, we'd conspire before a spanking was coming and fake cry while Mom spanked us. After she left the room, we'd quietly giggle together.

Mom may have been gentle and quiet, but she was a work-horse. Unlike Apu, I'd rarely see Mom sitting on the couch watching television. When she wasn't tending to the matters of the building, she was preparing food, cleaning the bird cage, doing laundry, mending Apu's well-worn work clothes, or cleaning the apartment.

Not only was I blessed to have flavourful Hungarian dishes coming from the hands of Apu, but I also had authentic German meals made by Mom's skilled hands: Rouladen, Goulash, Spaetzle, and Dampfnudel were feasts for my senses and for those walking in the hallway outside of our humble apartment.

Dinnertime was something we always did together. But as our mouths chewed, our eyes and attention were glued to the television, satisfying our addiction to *The Young and the Restless*—the four of us were enamoured with that daytime soap opera, which we watched for many years.

We ate together, and we also worked together. At a young age, I was expected to contribute to the maintenance of Wyndham Place. Angelina and I worked hard in that six-storey, seventy-two-unit building. Our regular chores included slipping rent notices and receipts under apartment doors, vacuuming hallways, mopping stairwells, changing burnt light bulbs, washing light covers in the hallways, washing windows, washing walls, shoveling sidewalks, and scraping wallpaper from vacant units. I also helped Apu shovel garbage into the giant incinerator—I'm talking Freddy Krueger style scary basement incinerator—that was situated across from the massive hot water boiler for the building.

Angelina and I not only worked together, we also played together along with the other kids who lived in the building. We'd usually be found in the park and when we heard the tune from ice cream truck drawing near, we'd sprint to the patio of our building and holler for Mom to throw down money. When it was time for us to come in for dinner, Mom would give a wickedly loud whistle using her thumb and forefinger to summon us. After dinner, we'd walk to local pool for a cool swim, and afterwards, we'd come home and eat cold watermelon before getting ready for our early bedtime. In the dark and cold winters, we'd go tobogganing together on the double-decker hill by our school. Before settling in for sleep, we'd tickle each other's arms from our bunk beds. Angelina would dangle her arm down while I propped mine up. We took turns over who got to go last, and we'd quietly count to ensure we got the same tickle time. I usually cheated.

A Normal Life

I considered my childhood to be "normal." I had a mom, a dad, and a sister. I also had a range of pets through the years. We always had a cockatiel, who was always named Conrad. And Angelina and I rotated through pet rodents, including a dwarf rabbit (Madonna), a chinchilla (Lorenzo), a number of gerbils (Woodchuck, Woodstock, Cindy, and Mustard), and a baby grey squirrel (yes, a squirrel) named Walter. I loved animals so much that I aspired to be a veterinarian.

But I digress.

So, yes. Childhood. Normal. I had a family and I had pets. I went to school. I played with my friends. I played in the banana-slide park by the apartment. And I did my chores, with some complaining and resisting.

Aside from eating family meals and contributing to the maintenance of the building, we did fun family things together too. Each December, Angelina and I would snuggle in blankets in the back of Apu's brown Chrysler station wagon for the long drive into the country, where we'd hunt in knee-deep snow for the perfect Christmas tree to cut. And in the back of that same station wagon, we'd spend evenings eating popcorn and watching movies at the local drive-in theatre.

My version of a normal childhood also included seeing the delicate pale skin around my mom's blue eyes swollen and bruised from the occasional blows she'd receive to her face. She tried to hide her injuries by wearing sunglasses in the apartment, but this didn't ease the blow to my psyche, even with Corey Hart's *Sunglasses at Night* making it okay.

Normal also meant seeing Angelina's lips swell and bleed after getting back-handed by Apu's thick hands at the kitchen table when he didn't like what she was saying.

Each time I saw a sign of violence, I'd feel a pang of unease in my stomach and a tightness in my chest. I loved my family immensely, but the things that I was seeing and the unease that I was feeling didn't make sense to me. And despite my inseparable relationship with my sister, and my mom's open and loving nature, we never talked of what happened.

Unlike my sister who spoke up for herself, I began to hide, and it became normal for me so that I could avoid seeing the things that confused and hurt me. It also meant quieting my voice and stifling my opinion so that I didn't end up with swollen and bleeding lips or black eyes.

But hiding in my room, under the bed, or behind the curtains didn't stop me from seeing the things that hurt me. There were signs of violence that didn't fade like the bruises on my mom's face. The broken glass door in the living room wall unit, the bullet holes in my parents' dresser, and the etched scars from smashed dishes in the kitchen floor were subtle and persistent reminders that prevented me from feeling truly safe in my home.

I soon earned the nickname of "Mousie," which family and close family friends would call me for many years to come—around forty of them. Although I had become a quiet and shy girl who tried to please my parents, getting spanked at the end of Apu's outbursts was unavoidable. After all, I was still a kid who'd watch television rather than do chores, make prank calls on the rotary phone rather than do homework, and stay home and play with my gerbils rather than visit with my aunt and cousins, which we did almost every weekend.

One Sunday before heading to my aunt's house, Angelina and I were playing with our gerbils. My parents were ready to leave, and naturally, Angelina and I were in no rush. Apu started getting annoyed and angry. I tried to collect our gerbils that were scurrying about on the carpet in the hallway of our apartment, but those little guys were quick. Apu's impatience escalated, as did my panic. Through my desperate and hastened efforts to collect our little pets, I stumbled and fell. As I landed, I felt Mustard's little skull crush beneath my knee. A part of me crushed right along with it. I sobbed hysterically. I had just killed an animal. And to boot, I had upset Angelina—Mustard was her gerbil.

Note to Self: Oh, Love. I know you feel so bad right now, and it's okay to feel that way! It wasn't your fault. Just know that the little guy felt no pain and went straight to heaven. He had no hard feelings. Pretty sure Angelina is over it too.

On another occasion getting ready to go out as a family, Apu was growing impatient at my sloth-like speed. I was finally ready, but I had to pee badly, and I wanted to do so before getting in the car. Apu's temper started boiling over and I bolted for the bathroom, quickly locking the door behind me before sitting on the toilet. Thrashing sounds of Apu's fists pounding on the bathroom door startled me from the seat. I didn't know if I should pull my pants up or finish peeing.

Panic and terror filled me. Through my sobs and the pounding door, I managed to shout, "I really need to pee."

To my relief, the thrashing came to an abrupt stop, but the sound of pounding fists and splitting wood and the feeling of terror were deeply etched into my long-term memory.

A Twinkle of Hope

Life moved on at Wyndham Place, where tenants came and tenants went, and where we remained planted as a happy family. You see, despite the anger and signs of violence I had seen, I felt we had a "happy" family. Seeing evidence of violence struck a chord of discomfort and restlessness in me, but I quickly disregarded my feelings of unease and instead normalized the violence and accepted it as the way life was. It helped that my mom managed to hide and suppress her anguish and provided tender love to my sister and me, regardless of what she was experiencing. And Apu was equally as loving toward us, in his own ways.

Mom had vowed to herself to remain in her relationship with Apu—no matter what—to ensure that my sister and I would have a stable home while we were young and dependent. But soon enough, Mom found a fresh source of happiness when a family with two young boys, of similar ages to me and Angelina, moved into the building. The dad and husband, Marcus, was a tall, dark, and handsome Italian man. Mom and Marcus instantly fell in love—at first sight.

Our two families spent a lot of time together. Marcus became best friends with Apu, and I became best friends with the older boy. And the more time our families spent together, the stronger the love and the connection between Mom and Marcus grew. To maximize their time together, they'd meet at the grocery store and in the corners of the moth-scented, ground floor locker room to share a loving handhold or a gentle kiss. Mom felt solace in those short moments when she could confide in Marcus of the torment she had endured living under the strong hand of Apu.

Despite Mom and Marcus' efforts at cloaking their love for one another, Apu caught sight of some flirty glances and became suspicious. Although I saw the bullet holes in the dresser, saw black eyes more frequently, and heard Hungarian music more often, I was oblivious to the severe torment that my mom had endured.

Much later in my life, I learned from Mom that Apu had pointed a gun at her. And on another occasion, he had wrapped his leathery hands around her delicate neck. Her feet dangled in the air, while Apu uttered that he'd kill her if she ever left him, because if he couldn't have her, then no one could. I also learned that in a fit of rage Apu had attempted to burn down the building by lighting newspapers on fire and dropping them into the garbage chutes.

With tension escalating, Marcus and his family moved out of Wyndham Place. Before leaving, Marcus reminded Mom to follow her heart. And with that, the little twinkle that had risen in Mom's eyes and wide smile, had also left.

The apartment had become a prison for Mom, and I believed that this was the way life was supposed to be. It was normal.

My First Love

To escape the arduous labour of working in the building, I started working as Apu's assistant floor sander. The job was more physically demanding than the chores I had done around the building, and I had to wake up super early, but Apu paid me well. I also got a job delivering thick Sears Catalogues—hundreds of which I lugged around in my rickety buggy in, through, and around apartment buildings in the area. I would crank that buggy up flights of stairs where there were no elevators, determined and committed to get the job done. That job wasn't any easier than being the superintendent's little helper either, but at least I earned some money from it.

I got my first "real" job at a fast food restaurant. It's funny (actually, not really), having a manager make blatant sexual advances toward under-aged girl employees seemed acceptable in the 1980s. I didn't know any different. After late-night shifts, the manager let me drive his cool white Pontiac Firebird home. Aside from spin-the-bottle in grade six, my first experience of romance was making out with my manager in those burgundy leather seats while parked in front of my building at two in the morning. He tried his hardest to get his greasy (no pun intended) hands into my starchy uniform pants. Despite conflicting feelings of obligation and being grossed out, I managed to stave him off, and he never got the satisfaction he so desperately sought. At least not with this employee.

> *Note to Self:* Girl, that's workplace sexual harassment. Not acceptable. Report it.

I took a liking to Nico—one of the regular customers at the restaurant. He lived down the street in a youth group home. Every shift I worked, Nico was there ordering food and striking up a conversation with me while I worked. And during my breaks, he would sit and talk with me as I'd eat. Nico was handsome. He was slightly taller than me, and he was tanned and well-built from working outside as a landscaper.

Having served his time at the group home for his crime of theft, Nico moved back into his parent's home, which was a solid one-and-a-half-hour bus ride from my apartment. Nico and I saw more and more of each other, and I became a frequent guest in his parents' place. Although his parents spoke Greek with little knowledge of English, they welcomed me with open arms and treated me like their daughter. They adored me, and I adored their warmth and their Greek cooking.

Although I didn't feel any warm fuzzy feelings, saying "I love you" seemed like the thing to do. And so, I "loved" Nico. Much of my time outside of school and work was spent with Nico. And although he didn't come into work as often since he lived back home with his parents, he usually bussed home with me after work. But on one warm summer night, instead of taking the bus from the subway, we walked through the dark, desolate field surrounding the subway station. And there, at the age of fifteen, on a hill of prickly, dried grass, I succumbed to Nico's constant pressures to have sex. Like the empty love that I felt for Nico, intercourse was much the same—without any feeling. Anaesthetized, I went through the motions of what I perceived to be my responsibility and the thing I should do as a girlfriend in love.

As time passed, Nico became controlling, aggressive, and extremely jealous of other guys who looked at me or talked to me. It wasn't long before Nico's verbal aggression transitioned to physical aggression. The first punch came when he bussed me home after work one night. As we arrived at my building, we stood on the double-decker hill in the dark. I don't recall what set him off, but I was entirely unsuspecting of what was about to come my way. I gasped to catch my breath as I hunched over from the fist that had plowed into my stomach. I was bewildered as to what had just happened to me. Other times, I'd receive punches to the side of my head or torso while he was driving or while we were walking in the dark. And each time he'd punch me, I'd be confused and quiet. Violence was common in my childhood home, so I took it as the way things were supposed to be. It was my normal. It didn't feel good, but it was comforting and reassuring, in a distorted sense. So, I continued to love Nico.

Sex continued to be something I did out of obligation. Much like his cigarette addiction, sex was an outlet for Nico; an alternative punching bag. Nico expected to have sex numerous times every time we were together, regardless of whether I wanted to or not. I thought this expectation was normal and a part of all relationships. But something didn't feel right. Something within me knew that forced and obligatory sex was wrong. I could sense it in every part of me. My body gave signs through its aching and bleeding. Yet, day in and day out and repeatedly therein, I continued to silence my voice and my body, and I succumbed to Nico's force and aggression and lie there for him, waiting and wondering when he'd finally get his fix.

I was thrilled to take a step up from the sexually-harassing, greasy job at the fast food place and landed a job working in the deli department at a fine food market, which was a convenient five-minute walk from my high school. The brightly lit store with large, front windows made it easy for Nico to monitor my every move from across the street, where he sat and waited for me to finish work. As I was wrapping things up from my first shift, Nico entered the store and yelled profanities and accusations at my male co-workers for, what Nico believed was, hitting on me.

WTF. My *first* day at my new job! Like, seriously?! I was not impressed.

I had worn Nico's over-sized leather coat since we had started dating, because it made me feel cool and tough, perhaps to compensate for the fear I was constantly suppressing at home without even knowing. But that September evening after work was mild, so I draped the coat over my forearm as Nico and I walked home. Nico rambled incessantly with non-sensical accusations, revolving around me talking to my co-workers. No matter which way I looked at it, my mind could not justify his outburst at my place of work as being okay. It felt wrong.

After roughly twenty minutes of listening to Nico's nonsense and pleading with him to understand that I *had* to talk to my co-workers, even if they were male, I finally had enough. As we rounded a corner in the road, I stopped and gently placed my coat over a fire hydrant. And then, without planning or thinking, I reeled my arm back with a clenched fist, and I let it fly—straight and square into the middle of Nico's face. Blood gushed out of his now-broken-nose and he squinted to see from his quickly blackening eyes. There was no retaliation from Nico—he was either in too much pain or too much shock. Perhaps both.

Although violence was not uncommon in my home, I had never been violent myself. I was far too timid and quiet to be aggressive, and I didn't like violence. But, admittedly, that was a proud moment for me.

We arrived at my place, and I drove Nico home in my mom's car. I did feel slightly bad at the time. Just slightly.

> *Note to Self:* Don't date guys who've committed a crime and live in a group home, even if they're tanned and cute. Unless, of course, they've done their inner work.

The Great Escape

With a strong love of animals, I started working at a pet store when I was in grade thirteen. It was a step up from the deli and in-line with my love of animals and aspiring career as a veterinarian. Along with that change, came news of my acceptance to the University of Guelph, where I would begin my studies toward my dream career.

Or not.

I began making plans to move away from home, my family, and my first love and his fists. Although I was moving over an hour away, Nico and I remained together in a long-distance relationship. But the physical distance between us and the newness of my surroundings brought relief and realizations for me; I began to distance myself from Nico emotionally and slowly sever my enmeshment with him. Although I was still his girlfriend, I began to feel lighter and freer in the absence of regular contact with him.

My escape to university brought possibility into my life, and it opened the door to my freedom. And while I was engrossed and enjoying the newness of my surroundings, Mom was making her own plan of escape.

Mom's vow to herself was being fulfilled—her girls were on their way to becoming independent, young adults. Angelina had a steady boyfriend and was well into her university program, and I was moving out to begin mine.

Although Mom's heart ached and longed to be with Marcus, the rest of her body trembled with fear at the thought of leaving Apu. Apu had given Mom ample tastes of what would happen if she left him. So, she played the part of prisoner-wife while she stealthily began to plan her great escape.

Aware of Mom's love for Marcus, Apu was on strict watch—he bugged the phones and locked up the car key. But Mom was determined, and there were moments in her days when the chains loosened slightly. Apu would abandon his close watch over her when he'd leave the building to go to work. It was during those times that Mom conspired with close friends in the building to plan her escape.

One unsuspecting day, Mom mustered all her courage and reported Apu's threats and abuse to the police. One of Mom's friends followed Apu and confirmed that he was at a jobsite, while another friend awaited Mom in an escape car. Within a matter of minutes, Mom hastily packed twenty years of her life in a couple of bags and fled for her life.

A Shattered Home

When I learned of Mom's escape from the friends that covertly assisted her, I was bewildered and in disbelief. I refused to accept that my family had been shattered. I was even more alarmed and confused to learn that Mom would not share her location with my sister and me.

Soon after, Mom established contact with Angelina and me, and we arranged to meet at an unfamiliar restaurant in Toronto. So, on a weekend I bussed home from Guelph to unite with my fragmented family. It was like a reunion scene from the movies, except in this scene, the daughters didn't run toward the mother colliding in a loving embrace. Instead, the confused daughters warily approached the mother, fraught with bitterness and feelings of abandonment.

As we settled into the burgundy, fake-leather seats of the window-booth, Mom informed us that she was now living with Marcus in a small condominium apartment. Unaware of her secret love affair for all the years and the extent of the physical abuse she had endured with Apu, I was instantly furious over Mom's betrayal of our family.

Mom continued to explain that Apu was violent toward her and that she was worried that he would kill her if he found her, and that this is the reason she refrained from telling us where she was now living. Despite Mom's sincere and heartfelt words, I rejected the idea of Mom and Marcus being together. At that moment, I felt Marcus was the instigator who tore apart my happy family. Yes, even with the signs of violence that my innocent and unsuspecting young eyes had seen, I detested that my happy family was now broken.

Even with the disappointment that I was showing in that booth, and despite the extreme abuse from Apu that Mom had endured, Mom never defended her actions by painting a poor picture of Apu. She let me keep my personally formed opinions of him that I had developed from what I saw and experienced living with him at Wyndham Place. It was this same gracious approach I would employ later in my life, as I watched my own daughter form her own opinions of her father.

Summer faithfully returned, and with it came the end of my residency on campus and my return "home." With stuffed animals and pillow in hand, I returned to an apartment void of love and security. In place of Mom's loving presence, was a dad that I barely recognized. Apu had replaced his inherited responsibilities of superintendent with late-night partying and daytime sleeping.

Apu had a new girlfriend, Linda-the-Lush as I coined her back then. She was a harsh woman with a raspy voice and breath that wreaked of alcohol. She referred to everyone as, "Honey" in a derogatory, high-pitched nasally tone. She swore frequently in regular conversation, something which was as unfamiliar to me as the tattoo that Apu now had etched on his arm. Linda was in the apartment often, and we constantly argued over the care of Shadow (our sweet Miniature Poodle that I had brought home from the pet store) and over the responsibilities in the building, which were being shirked by Apu.

It's thanks to Linda, that I have gained stunt-double experience. I had finished a shift at the pet store one afternoon, and Apu was driving me home. As he rounded the corner approaching Wyndham Place, he dropped a bomb and declared that Linda was moving into the apartment. With denial and anguish, and the car still moving, I flung open the door and dropped out of the car. My body stopped rolling when it landed in the belly of a gravel ditch. My physical pain was quickly numbed and replaced with emotional pain, and without rational thought, I sprinted into the apartment and screamed with rage, for the first time in my life, at Linda.

Still rejecting Mom and Marcus' relationship and feeling I had no other place to go, I planned to move my things into Nico's place to live with his family for the summer. After all, they adored me, and putting up with repeated punches and forced sex from Nico seemed like a small price to pay in exchange for shelter and warm food. More importantly, their home would provide me with an escape from the emotional pain and feelings of abandonment and betrayal that surfaced within me when I was in the apartment—the place I used to call home.

Likewise, Angelina was making plans to move out of our upside-down childhood apartment as well. She had been dating a guy steadily but was arranging to move into her best friend's parents' house. And when she learned of my intent to move into Nico's home, she insisted we stick together to salvage what little of our family remained—just her and me. So, together we were welcomed with open arms into a loving family and their house, which we were encouraged to call home. But my whole concept of home was turned upside down, shattered, and completely dissolved. No more sawdust hugs. No more Christmas tree cutting. No more cabbage rolls or Goulash. No more *Young and the Restless*. No more snuggles on the couch with Apu. No more loving arm-tickling nestled in beside Mom's lap.

Acceptance

Over the summer, I began to visit regularly with Mom and Marcus at their new place. I saw a twinkle reemerge in Mom's eyes. And through honest conversations and seeing the loving relationship Mom and Marcus were now openly displaying, Marcus proved his love for Mom. I began to trust Marcus, understand Mom's decisions, and accept their relationship. I came to see Marcus as Mom's knight in shining armour. He provided the impetus Mom needed—the safety, security, and love that we all seek—that helped her to face her greatest fear and make the scary decision to leave violence and abuse.

I enjoyed time spent with Marcus and Mom in their small, one-bedroom, apartment—especially since Shadow now lived with them. I was always lovingly welcomed to stay with them, despite their limited space. Yet, I continued to return to my "home" where my sister and I were staying. Although Nico and I were still together, we did not see each other as often. We hung out together at various places for short periods of time, but I was no longer feeling as attached to him as I had before I left for university. The cycle of abuse was beginning to fade.

I maintained contact with Apu, who broke up with Linda and started dating Lisa—a woman who was addicted to crack cocaine. Lisa had a gentler personality, and from the times that I saw her, I rather liked her; we got along well. With his new lifestyle, Apu could no longer maintain his superintendent responsibilities, so a motel room served as their home until their baby came along, at which point they moved into an apartment building across the street from Wyndham Place.

Apu helped me move back to school that September, and when I arrived and settled in, I solemnly proclaimed to myself that I would never return home. I realized that creating a home was now up to me. With that acceptance and declaration, came a sense of personal empowerment. And in my second year of university, I started to accept offers from guys to meet for coffee, hang out at the university center, or watch television together. These guys were attractive and intelligent—and they didn't yell at me or punch me.

After almost six years of dating Nico, I removed the small, gold diamond promise ring that I had worn on my wedding finger, and I broke up with him.

What does one do with broken-promise rings?

Despite the abusive, degrading, and deprecating relationship, I suffered heartache and cried for many nights after the break-up. I played sappy songs from *Air Supply* to stimulate my tears and wallow in my pain and suffering.

But I got over it… we humans are resilient like that.

I transitioned into a new phase of my journey—one where I would sift and sort through life led by engrained experiences and buried beliefs which had formed during my "normal" childhood and clouded my sense of wholeness and happiness.

CHAPTER 2

Sifting and Sorting: Recycling the Past

Every problem contains within itself the seeds of its own solution.
—Norman Vincent Peale

L ike my idea of home had been shattered, so was my vision of becoming a veterinarian. Out of thousands of university applicants across the country, the veterinary college only accepted one hundred students a year. With the sense of freedom I had felt in my frosh year and my discovery of pub night, studying to score grades of over ninety percent to compete with other first-year applicants was not appealing nor my priority. So, at the start of my second year into my bachelor program, I sadly abandoned my dream of becoming a veterinarian and I began to specialize in Human Biology and Nutritional Sciences.

Years passed as I enjoyed a balance of attending classes, doing homework, socializing at the bars, and dancing at the clubs. I met great friends and dated great guys. I worked out at the campus fitness center and became certified as a fitness instructor to supplement my income and keep fit at the same time. I also worked as a cashier at a grocery store.

My fourth and final year of my university program approached without warning. Life was exciting, enjoyable, and entertaining, and I didn't want the experience to end! I had no clue as to what I wanted to be or do when I grew up. I wasn't ready for the working world. In fact, I was downright petrified at the thought of having to work and earn money to survive. I was content receiving government grants and loans and remaining in the safe confines of the educational system. So, at the end of my Bachelor of Science degree, I entered a Master of Science program.

When in doubt, stay in school.

A lot of hard work and time went into my postgraduate work, and a lot of fun and partying as well. My advisor was understanding and easy going, and the people that worked in my lab and the adjacent labs were down-to-earth, relatable, and active. We became a close-knit group of friends that did everything together from working in the lab and chatting at coffee breaks to playing sports, partying, and taking weekend trips to cottages.

In the meantime, Angelina married the man she had been steadily dating and they began a life together in downtown Toronto. Angelina's husband was loving and supportive of not only Angelina, but of me as well. I delighted in the life that my sister was building for herself, but at the same time reality began to hit as I neared completion of my second year of research and lab work. I questioned what I was going to do with my life and where it was headed. It felt like it was time for me to grow up. And it was scary.

With the close of my research, I moved into the safety of a basement bachelor apartment in Angelina's house. With newborn twins in their lives, I helped Angelina and her husband around the house. And between playing nanny and roller-blading twenty kilometers a day on the lakefront, I finished writing my thesis and completed my master's requirements.

Great! I had a Master of Science degree. *Now what?*

Mister Right

During my postgraduate studies, I had enjoyed being a teaching assistant for my advisor, but I didn't know what to do with that nor what career to pursue. What I knew for sure though, was what I *didn't* want to do: work in a lab and give baby rats cancer, starve them through a zinc-deficient diet, decapitate them, and then rip their warm livers out of their twitching and bloody bodies.

Note to Self: When in doubt, go on vacation!

Still riding out grants from my postgraduate studies, I rented a van with two girlfriends, and we headed to the East Coast of Canada for two weeks. The three of us drove and camped our way through the picturesque Maritime provinces enjoying a balance of outdoor activities, relaxing, and partying. Our final province was Prince Edward Island, and it was there, in an unassuming campground, that the path of my life changed.

A few campsites down from ours was a rowdy group of about twenty guys. Naturally, as single, young adult women, we found our way to their campsite. Eventually, our boisterous party relocated to the beach, where we drank, talked, and laughed for hours.

Turns out, these guys were all in massage therapy school a mere twenty-minute drive from where I was staying at my sister's place. Imagine that.

One tall and quirky guy, Paul, stood out from the group. Fair-skinned and light-haired, Paul wasn't the type to which I was typically attracted. But we connected instantly, and I was completely enchanted.

By the end of the day, Paul and I were becoming affectionate, and we had our first kiss right on the beach, just as a double rainbow appeared.

Surely this was a sign! I mean, meeting someone local to where I lived when I was almost two thousand miles from home?

And a double rainbow?

The next morning, we exchanged numbers with our new friends, and we made our way back home with our van slathered in red mud and our minds etched with precious memories to last a lifetime.

Although somewhat skeptical, my family was happy that I had met Mister Right. Paul and I started dating immediately. I loved his light-hearted approach, his humour, and his sense of fun. When my family met him, they approved instantly. We were two young adults in love, and I was convinced that he was the man that I would marry.

A Dream Come True

When Paul graduated from his massage therapy program, we backpacked in Africa. Our adventure started with an organized safari group that launched from Johannesburg, South Africa. We journeyed with a group of fourteen travelers and made our way through Zimbabwe, Botswana, Zambia, Malawi, Tanzania, Zanzibar, and Kenya.

As I had always dreamed of visiting Africa while watching nature shows with Apu, memories of sitting on the couch with him flashed through my mind during our guided open-topped bumpy safaris. It was everything I had dreamed of as a child. My eyes widened to fully capture the beauty and wonder, while the rest of my senses absorbed and internalized every detail of the foreign and surreal surroundings. I reveled without words as gazelle, antelope, giraffes, elephants, and rhinoceros collected and settled as one family at the murky watering hole. As dusk settled, each took a turn and yielded respectfully to the other in an unspoken governmental hierarchy of honour.

Bird songs filled the warm air from dawn to dusk each day, regardless of where we were. Warthogs and monkeys scampered about like bustling squirrels in an urban city. On Lake Malawi, we canoed into uncharted territory for two days where we had a terrifyingly close encounter with a hippopotamus. And while in our camp, we hushed and stood aside as majestic elephants swiftly strolled through our tents. Further excitement was added when we explored the land by foot guided by natives carrying machine guns, and when Paul and I bungee jumped over Victoria Falls.

While spending twenty-four hours a day in a foreign land with Paul, I began to see a side of him that I hadn't seen before. He frequently wanted to be alone, and when the situation didn't present such an opportunity, he became visibly edgy, irritable, and grumpy. His behaviour seemed to be related to something more than the personality trait of an introvert. This new side of Paul struck me as odd—and not a cute odd. But I dismissed Paul's behaviour and attributed it to our unusual surroundings and the numerous people we were consistently with in overly cozy living arrangements.

During the second-half of our trip, I often explored on my own while Paul stayed behind to recharge and relax in seclusion. With such diverse surroundings, it was easy to overlook Paul's preferences to be alone and get swept up in the beautiful scenery instead.

We concluded our adventure in the vast auburn deserts of Namibia and the lush landscape (and the penguins and seals) of Cape Town.

After nine amazing weeks, we returned to Toronto. I quickly dismissed any uneasy feelings I had about Paul and his need to isolate himself. I was determined that Paul was going to be the man that I married. He was smart and cute, *and* he didn't hit me. What a score!

I set my mind on the goal of marriage, and nothing was going to interfere with it.

> *Note to Self:* Oh, Girl. If only you knew how to listen and accept the signs that life is giving you. You'll figure it out. It's all good.

Happily Ever After

Shortly after our return from Africa, Paul's parents bought him an existing wellness clinic in a small city ninety-minutes from Toronto. There, we moved into an apartment and started building a life together. And life in our bright, clean, and cozy apartment was great! It was everything I had hoped for. It was home! And when Paul proposed, I was thrilled! My happily ever after with Paul was going just as I had planned.

Soon after we moved in, we adopted an ex-racing greyhound, Eros. Ever since leaving Shadow when I was in university, I wanted so desperately to have another dog. Eros was a gentle, docile, and quiet giant who needed to be taught to walk up and down stairs. We bonded instantly, and he was a wonderful addition to our home.

I was happy that Paul's career was off to a great start, but my happiness was overshadowed by feelings of pity and sorrow for myself. I continued to work for the grocery store where I had worked as a cashier in university, except now I was a corporate trainer in their head office. I travelled to franchises throughout Southwestern Ontario to hire and train their staff. Despite enjoying the work and the wonderful people with whom I worked, I felt empty. And seeing Paul so passionate about his work, magnified the lack of fulfillment I was feeling in my career.

Something was missing.

I came across a job posting for a manager of a retail nutrition store in the solitary mall in the city. I was passionate about health and nutrition, so I expected this job to be *the* job for me. I applied and was hired. Finally, my career calling!

Or not.

Within three months of starting my new job, I quit. Retail was not my thing. I couldn't be paid enough money to tolerate the long days in the store, which seemed to drag on forever. My shifts were mostly void of human interaction, filled only with bottles of supplements and music from *Gypsy Kings* echoing through the empty store.

Paul's income was enough to carry the rent and expenses, so I happily became the householder responsible for the shopping, cooking, laundry, cleaning, and walking Eros while trying to figure out what the heck I wanted to do as a career. I had seven years of post-secondary education and held many unrelated positions, yet none satisfied my deep yearning.

I couldn't put a finger on what this yearning was. I just knew I didn't feel fulfilled. There was something more to life that I was missing and in its place was a feeling of emptiness and confusion.

I considered going back to school to become a nutritionist since I was so passionate about living a healthy lifestyle, but I decided against it as I quickly landed job interviews thanks to the ample work experience and beefy education on my resume. These interviews inadvertently became personal career coaching sessions. I even cried in one interview for a personal trainer position at a health club, as the interviewer tried to help me pinpoint a career that would align with my background and my affinity for health sciences.

With no success in finding a job, I had the freedom to start a new hobby. Up to this point, reading had been limited to the things I *had* to read for school, mainly textbooks and scientific journals. I had no idea that reading was something people did for fun and enjoyment! I quickly got hooked after I dove into *Conversations with God*, by Neile Donald Walsh, which Paul had finished reading and handed to me.

I instantly consumed this book and craved more. Reading it felt like drinking water after being in the desert for a week. It quenched a thirst that I didn't even know I had. It felt good.

After I devoured the entire *Conversations with God* series, I studied work by Deepak Chopra, starting with *The Seven Spiritual Laws of Success* and *Quantum Healing*. Following that was work by Wayne Dyer.

With our wedding date set, my reading subsided and my quest for the perfect job turned into a quest for the perfect wedding. And within a few months, I discovered that I was pregnant! Life was really coming together—exactly as I had planned! Paul continued to work and bring home money to pay the bills, while I spent my days walking Eros, visiting the local health food store, planning the perfect wedding, and planning to be the perfect mom.

Life was awesome.

Until it wasn't.

Things with Paul changed. That side of him that I first saw during our time in Africa—the side I wasn't particularly fond of—reared its head again. When he came home for lunch, he would head straight into the bedroom and shut the door behind him. He appeared frazzled and agitated; he said he wanted alone time to unwind before heading back to the office for the afternoon.

This need for alone time also seeped into our evenings. Paul would spend hours reading multitudes of online spiritual literature, which, to me, seemed foreign and almost cult-like. But he was passionate about it and I gave him the space to do what made him happy.

I began having this deep gut feeling that maybe, just maybe, this wasn't the guy for me. But my mind quickly shut down and denied this feeling and inner knowing.

> *Note to Self:* Girl, listen to the hunches.
> They're never wrong.

Nope. This was it. This was my happily ever after. We were getting married. We were having a baby. I was going to be happy with Paul and have my perfect family. I was going to make it happen. I was determined. And when I caught Paul and his female friend exchanging flirty glances at a party, I was worried that my plan was spoiled, but it made me that much more determined to make this marriage happen.

Time elapsed and we grew emotionally distant from one another. We were still amicable and pleasant, but there was next to no connection between us other than running a business of cohabitating. A couple of times, we had discussed calling the wedding off, but the invitations were out. You can't call off a wedding once the invitations are out, right?

> *Note to Self:* Ah, yes you can, Christine.

Our wedding was beautiful. It was held a few hours north of Toronto at a lush and charming resort. With *Pachelbel's Canon* echoing in the fresh air, Apu escorted me in my curvy ivory gown and floral head band to the spot where Paul awaited.

We said our vows with a lake behind us and grass under our feet. It was perfect.

Almost.

Our vows were accompanied with strong winds, and wind was my least favourite element. To me, the gale force simply confirmed my deep inner knowing—it wasn't meant to be. So instead of crying with joy and love at my wedding, I sobbed from the inner turmoil I felt. It was more than cold feet; deep down I knew I shouldn't be marrying Paul.

During our speeches, we announced that in six months, we would be a family of three. The silent pause and dropped jaws proved we were successful in keeping our news a secret, even with our close families and friends. Our first dance, a Samba that Paul and I had taken lessons for, turned out perfect. I danced to *What a Wonderful World* with Apu. And get this, even Mom and Apu danced together. It was the first time since Mom fled the apartment for her life that she had seen Apu. But they put their differences aside for the sake of their daughter. It brought tears to Angelina's and my eyes. It was like a dream come true and a moment that we treasured deeply.

It was perfect.

After our big night, Paul revealed that our surprise honeymoon was a week at a meditation retreat, the caveat being that I had to drive the nine hours there. Paul's car was unreliable, and he didn't know how to drive my little black Honda Civic *Si* coupe because it was a stick shift. Our destination was a large and beautiful retreat intended for individuals to get in touch with themselves. Most activities Paul signed up for were meant to be done alone and in silence—not your typical honeymoon destination.

So, we spent the first week of our marriage mostly in silence apart from each other. It set the stage for our marriage.

Life back in our perfect home continued as it did before the marriage. Paul worked and then isolated himself when he was home. We were entirely pleasant with each other and talked openly and honestly, but the sense of a deep connection was missing. He shared with me one of the revelations he had during his time spent in contemplation.

He felt the baby was not his—it was an immaculate conception.

What does a wife say when her husband says this to her?

With disbelief, I disregarded the comment and continued to plan to have the perfect birth and to be the perfect mom.

> *Note to Self:* The only thing blinder than love is our attachment to our wants. Let go of those attachments, Girl!

The Perfect Birth

I thoroughly enjoyed being pregnant. Aside from mild nausea during the first three months, I felt fantastic. I was so in love with my baby as it grew in my belly. I couldn't wait to meet Baby, adore him, and have him by my side twenty-four hours a day. You see, I was going to raise this baby using the Continuum Concept. I was never going to let Baby down. I wanted Baby to feel safe and secure, and to achieve this, I was going to carry Baby snuggled close to my body in a sling—all day, every day, and everywhere.

And the birth?

A home waterbirth with midwives.

Yup. That was the plan.

As my due date approached, an ultrasound revealed that Baby was breech. Unwilling to let go of my dream birth, I immediately began researching how to get breech babies to turn naturally. I ate certain foods, contorted my body in various positions, and placed headphones with symphony music blasting in my crotch (yes, my pants were on), to get Baby to turn, so I could have the perfect home birth.

I was past-due. And when I declined my midwife's advice to schedule a cesarean, they withdrew their services.

I was attached to my plan. I was determined to have a perfect home birth—even if that meant birthing the baby with just Paul and myself. And that's what we naively attempted to do. Paul researched and gathered supplies. And when contractions finally started one evening, we scurried in preparation.

My water broke after several hours of contractions. I was excited and scared. It was time for Baby to start descending. Except it wasn't Baby, it was his lifeline. His umbilical cord prolapsed, which meant oxygen could be cut off, and, yes, Baby could die.

Reality hit.

We were in over our heads.

> *Note to Self:* Oh, Girl. If I wasn't so loving and accepting,
> I'd be calling you an idiot right now and judging and
> cursing you for risking your sweet baby's life. What's done
> is done. I forgive you completely, and I love you despite
> your naïve and self-centered behaviours.

It was time to get this baby delivered by professionals. I hobbled into the back of Paul's new SUV and rested on my elbows and knees to help circumvent the effects of gravity to discourage Baby's descent. Within five minutes, we pulled into the hospital's emergency department.

The last thing I recall was lying on a bed with medical staff swarming around and asking me questions. I'm sure they were thinking, *This lady's an idiot.*

I awoke in agonizing pain, unable to utter anything other than "Ow." After a swift shot of morphine, the medical staff wheeled Baby beside my bed.

Paul and I instantly agreed to Baby's name after a vivid dream I had while I was pregnant. It was of an African woman giving birth to a child, and the name "Zeydan" stuck firmly and resolutely in my mind when I awoke from it.

Okay, I thought. *So, this is Zeydan? My baby? He's cute.*

I didn't feel the warm and fuzzy feelings I had anticipated over the past almost ten months. I stared blankly at all nine pounds and eleven ounces of him.

"Hi, Zeydan," I whispered to this little stranger beside me.

The nurses abruptly informed me that Zeydan had inhaled meconium and was having trouble breathing. And with that, they whisked him out of my room to transport him to a children's hospital for intensive care.

The operating doctor came into my room. Unamused, he informed me that he reported Paul and me to Family and Children's Services because of the foolish choices we had made as naïve expecting parents. I merely brushed off the doctor's words because the graveness of my actions had not yet occurred to me. I was still entirely attached to mind's wants for the birth of my baby.

Within hours, I was shipped to the children's hospital to reunite with Zeydan. I was stationed in a private room with a window in the maternity wing. When Paul arrived, we spent time with Zeydan in the intensive care unit. Zeydan's little fingers managed to grip mine through the numerous tubes that protruded from his nose, mouth, belly button, hands, and feet. The nurses explained that Zeydan was receiving a round of antibiotics to combat bacteria from the meconium and that he needed an aspirator to help him breathe.

While Zeydan recovered, I did much of the same.

Healing through a caesarian? Not so fun.

But the next day, my focus shifted from my recovery to Zeydan's, and I spent as much time with him as possible. Zeydan helped make that easier when he pulled the aspirator out of his mouth and breathed steadily and strongly without it.

He was transferred into the regular newborn unit in the maternity ward just down the hall from where I was stationed. And together we remained there while Zeydan's round of antibiotics completed. The nurses had tried finding veins in his body, but after repeated attempts of pinning him down and poking him, they started to aim for the noticeable vein in his forehead. I stayed by Zeydan's side trying to calm him as he fought, thrashed, and wailed from the assault to his hands and feet, but I couldn't bear to witness the attempts at the vein in his forehead. Instead, I waited outside the door, crouched and sobbing into my cupped hands while my son was tortured by these professionals who were doing their jobs for the sake of my son's health. The ordeal ended, and I was reunited with Zeydan who was now fitted with a small plastic cup taped to his shaved forehead to keep him from pulling out the needle and intravenous tube through which the medicine was now administered.

Days of the week passed slowly. When Zeydan was awake, I nursed him or simply held him. He nursed well and was already able to focus on objects with a stern and discerning glance. At almost ten pounds, he looked like he was two months old. Rounds of medical students regularly poked and prodded Zeydan, trying to find something to diagnose—but to no avail.

A week after Zeydan was born, we finally came home to begin our lives as a happy family.

Or not.

The Joy of Motherhood

Much like my vision of a peaceful, beautiful, and deeply intimate childbirth was utterly shattered, so was my vision of motherhood.

At least initially.

Here was this strange little human that I was entirely responsible for, twenty-four hours a day, without exception. I felt so much love for him during the pregnancy, but after the birth, I felt little connection.

My life as I had known it was completely shattered. I was devasted that I didn't have the enjoyable birthing experience to which I was so attached. I was in pain from the surgery and exhausted from nursing and caring for a newborn around the clock. Thankfully, other than having a hard time maintaining my milk supply, Zeydan and I had a solid nursing relationship.

What was that again? The Continuum Concept?

Ha!

When Zeydan cried, I didn't have the mental or emotional capacity to console him (never mind carry him around all day), other than to nurse him on demand.

I had envisioned and expected motherhood to be blissful, warm, and loving. For me, it was anything but. I cried every day in despair. It felt like I created a prison for which there was no escape.

> *Note to Self:* Oh, Girl. Welcome to Postpartum Depression. They never taught you this in school, but it's common after birth. It's okay to feel this way! You're doing the best you can with where you're at and what you know. I know it sucks. But this too shall pass!

Paul recognized my distress and did his best to help. When he wasn't working, he readily stepped in and comforted Zeydan when he cried. In seeing my struggle, Paul scheduled an appointment with an energy worker who helped heal families from traumatic births.

So, off we went. A few weeks after we got home, we ventured on our first trip out of the city as a family.

The energy healer first worked with each of us separately in a Reiki-like fashion. Nothing stood out for me in terms of what I experienced, but when she worked on us as a family, there were a lot of tears and sobbing. It was intimate. It was loving. It was powerful.

The next day was a new day for me—the start of a new life. My mental and emotional state had entirely turned around. I no longer felt despair and disdain for my role as a mother. In fact, I now *loved* it! I felt the secure, loving connection with Zeydan that I had while he was in my womb. I couldn't cuddle, kiss, or love him enough to satisfy the deep love I felt for him.

Yes. The joy of motherhood.

A Time of Change

Once my relationship with Zeydan got on track, my relationship with Paul returned to the status quo. We were still amicable and talked openly, but Paul spent much of his home time in solitude. Any connection between us had wholly dissipated. We didn't consider counselling, and we didn't tell our families of our troubles. It was evident and undeniable that neither of us wanted to be in the marriage any longer. So, when Zeydan was six months old, we declared our marriage over.

We announced our decision to our shocked families, as Paul made plans to rent an apartment nearby. Within a matter of weeks, Paul walked out the door with his few belongings.

After he left, I cleaned. I didn't cry or process any feelings until a few days after while on a massage table when the therapist asked me, "What's new?"

Note to Self: Yeah, you had some news! Let the floods come, Girl! Don't deny those feelings. Feel them!

I grieved the dissolution of our relationship and marriage. I worried about Zeydan not being raised in a real family. I mourned the loss of my perfect family—the loss of my happily ever after.

Paul and I swiftly processed the divorce and remained in an amicable relationship. He continued to work and had Zeydan for visits at his apartment on weekends. Paul generously supported me, so I could stay at home and care for Zeydan full-time. I thoroughly enjoyed my days of single motherhood that I filled with rollerblading with Zeydan in the stroller, visiting with my friend and her baby boy, biking with Zeydan strapped in a seat on the back of my bike, socializing at the Early Years center, and walking with Zeydan nestled in a sling on my body with Eros at my side. Aside from the pet and health food stores, the city's quaint and picturesque river was our usual destination.

Other than the dear superintendents of my apartment building who treated me like their own daughter, I had no friends or family in the city. So, when weekends arrived, I packed up and headed to Toronto to stay with Mom and Marcus in the house they had bought that conveniently had a spare room.

While in Toronto, Zeydan and I also visited with Apu. After Lisa's second child with Apu, she became engulfed in her crack addiction and incapable of functioning as a mother to her sons, and she left. With the help of his sister, Apu stepped up to the plate and was a dedicated dad to his two baby boys. He proved to be a caring father who took on full responsibility for his sons. During our visits, we would talk about diapers and poop while our sons played together.

Blissful single motherhood with Zeydan continued, and I enjoyed every moment of it. Zeydan's first birthday approached, and on the morning of his special day, I awoke from an early phone call. I groggily made out Angelina's phone number on the display. I picked up the phone, fully expecting to hear a cheery "Happy Birthday" for Zeydan's first birthday milestone.

Instead, I heard, "Apu died."

Only Angelina's faint sobs penetrated the silence, which seemed to persist for eternity.

In shock and disbelief, I managed to tremble out, "What? What do you mean?"

"Apu died in his sleep last night. He had a heart attack."

The phone dropped from my hands. My knees buckled beneath me, and I collapsed to the floor.

Unable to comprehend and process what my ears had just heard, nor control my body's reactions, I remained kneeling in a ball on the floor until my body began heaving in sobs of utter pain and unbearable anguish.

My mind could not comprehend the news I had just heard. Where was the "Happy Birthday" I was expecting to hear?

No more, "Hiya, Baby!" No more smoky sawdust hugs. Ever.

The rest of my son's first birthday was a blur. It was shrouded with a deep impression of emotional shock.

Unlike at Daddy's funeral, I couldn't repress or deny the pain or hold back the tears at Apu's funeral. I grieved the loss of my dad. I loved him. He was there for me, in his own special and unique way, throughout most of my life.

I was also saddened for my two young stepbrothers, who now had no mother or father and were left in the care of

Apu's sister and nephew. I've never seen or heard from my stepbrothers again.

Unlike Apu's life, my life back home continued. With our weekly trips to Mom and Marcus', Zeydan and I spent a lot of time with Angelina and her boys. Zeydan developed a strong bond with his twin cousins and enjoyed playing with them, while I enjoyed the extra help from my mom and sister.

In the meantime, Paul processed his own life changes. Without notice, he closed the doors of his healing center. He left his clients, staff, and office lease and worked as a temporary landscaper nearby before moving in with his parents. Within months, I received word that he was moving to western Canada to find himself, and that with these changes he was unable to continue providing financial support. So, before Zeydan turned two, I returned to the workforce. Following my earlier interest and enjoyment in teaching university students, I began teaching adults at a small learning center close to my apartment.

To help with my suddenly full schedule, Paul's parents lovingly adopted Eros and gave him a wonderful home and life. Paul's parents also generously paid child support when Paul could no longer afford to. Paul's parents adored Zeydan and were eager to see him and help, so for one weekend each month Zeydan stayed at their place.

My job at the learning center quickly evolved into a career. After teaching a variety of subjects and rocking at it, I was promoted to the position of manager. And within a matter of months, I started travelling an hour each way to manage a second small learning center in a neighbouring city. And after managing the two centers, I was transferred to Waterloo, where I managed a single, large learning center.

Strangely and unexpectedly, I enjoyed the work that I was doing—there was something in helping others learn that ignited a spark in me. For the first time in my life, I didn't plan, fret, force, or attach myself to an outcome. For the first time in my life, I felt passion for the work I was doing.

With half-day preschool quickly approaching, I was presented with the challenge of transporting Zeydan from the babysitter's to school in the middle of the day while I was almost an hour away.

The solution?

Move!

My dear boss suggested it. And with no family, friends, or work tying me to the city in which I lived, it took a matter of minutes for me to accept her suggestion. It made perfect sense. Within a couple months, we moved into a spacious two-bedroom apartment in Waterloo—literally down the street from where I worked and from where Zeydan was to start at his private preschool.

Recreating the Past

Around the time I was planning to move to Waterloo, a friend from my high school days emailed me. Years earlier, when I first met Seth, he was a cool sales clerk at the mall where I had worked at the pet store. He was tall, slender, dark-haired, and handsome. We hung out, drank, smoked up, and went clubbing as friends, but we had an unexplainable connection and mutual attraction. And despite Seth having a girlfriend, we enjoyed flirting with each other.

A few years after I had left for university, Seth and his girlfriend split, and he moved away. It had been about five years since I'd heard from him when I received that email from him out of the blue. In it, he said that he had been married, had a child, and separated, and he wanted to start dating me.

My response?

"Sure. If you clean up your act."

As a mom, my priorities had changed. I was no longer interested in partying. Sure, I enjoyed going to a club every so often to dance the night away with a few drinks, but the degree of partying I did in the past with Seth was not where I was currently at. Plus, I had a son and Seth wasn't a character that I wanted as a role model for Zeydan.

But oh no. You see, Seth was going to change. He said he was going to quit smoking because he was applying to become a firefighter. And it would be wonderful for Zeydan to have a father in his life, which he was clearly missing as he called his babysitter's husband, "Daddy."

Great! I thought. I accepted Seth's request, and we started dating.

> *Note to Self:* Don't date people based on who you want them to become or who they say they're going to be. Date them for who they are, and if you can't accept their character traits and habits as they are at that moment, then move on, Sister!

Seth lived in a dark and damp basement bedroom at his friend's place an hour away. He had no home and no job. His possessions included a run-down car, a duffle bag of clothes, a video game console with games, and an overly possessive rescue dog.

Seth spent a lot of time at my new apartment with Zeydan and me. And since Paul was still out west, Zeydan readily latched onto Seth as his male role model. Seth drove an hour each way to visit us in Waterloo, so it made perfect sense, at the time, to invite Seth to move in with us.

Note to Self: Girl, don't invite boyfriends with no job or credit rating to move in with you. Unless, of course, they've done their inner work.

Ever since our flirting days when I worked at the pet shop, Seth would secretly tell me that I was his dream girl. And now that we were finally together, he repeatedly told me that he wanted to spend the rest of his life with me. Our connection from the past remained strong, and I was utterly swept up in it. I fell head over heels in love with Seth.

Although Seth slept in every morning, I'd find charming love notes on my way out the door as I'd leave to drop off Zeydan at school and go to work. And when I got home from work and picking up Zeydan from school, the three of us went for bike rides and walks in the cemetery with Seth's dog (who now lived with us as well). The three of us had fun times together.

It felt like we were a real family.

Except…

Seth didn't keep to his promise of quitting smoking, and this left a bitter taste of betrayal and resentment in my mouth. Not only that, Seth smoked pot almost every time we were together. I was not interested in smoking up, especially with my motherly responsibilities. And I simply couldn't understand why this was something Seth wanted to do regularly. He said it was like having a beer. But I didn't drink beer—so, that didn't help me understand any better. Smoking pot was something I did when I was younger and didn't have a son. At this stage in my life, I simply did not want to get high.

Head over heels quickly faded into frustration. I worked full-time and cared for Zeydan. I did the cooking, cleaning, and laundry. Seth? He didn't. Although he worked as a school crossing guard for meager dollars a day, he didn't contribute in any manner to the maintenance of the household, other than having fun together with Zeydan and me. Not only did he not contribute financially to any living expenses, he quietly helped himself to my stash of twenty-dollar bills that I was saving in a pretty little box on my computer desk. And, in spite of my asking Seth not to play violent video games with Zeydan around, he did.

And the firefighter job Seth said he was going to get? That didn't happen. He didn't make it past the first interview.

Yes. Head over heels was long gone.

And I had had enough.

Enough of Seth's freeloading, his lack of contribution to the responsibilities in the home, and his disregard for my wishes.

I was done. It was time to break up.

Discussions took place. It wasn't easy—breaking up usually isn't. Seth and I both resisted. We shared a strong connection, and we loved each other. I was his dream girl, and I think deep down every girl wants to be a guy's dream girl just like in the fairytales.

But Seth was not my knight in shining armor. He was simply another dependent for me to care for and support.

I was convinced and determined. I stood firmly and decided to end the relationship.

But life had other plans.

Plan B

Note to Self: Don't rely on rhythm as a method of birth control.

I was pregnant.

Ugh!

My break up train veered off track.

With a baby on the way and Zeydan's adoration for Seth, my decision to stay in the relationship was an easy one to make... for the sake of the children.

Plus, Seth would be a dad, so, surely, he'd change his ways. We'd have a child that would bring us closer together. And with Zeydan, we'd be a family of four. We'd do fun things together. We'd fall head over heels in love again. And Seth would step up to responsibility like Apu finally did with his boys.

Or not.

Seth accepted that his career as a firefighter was not going to happen, so he switched to Plan B: heavy equipment operator. He would continue to work as a school crossing guard while earning the necessary licensing to operate heavy machinery.

With Plan B in place, we decided to buy a house. And in no time, we found the perfect one. You know when you know.

Built in 1932, our two-story brick home was adorned with original features, including the windows, doors, banisters, and hardwood floors. Prominent, dark-stained, and fine-detailed oak trim hugged the door and window frames, which were matched by equally as majestic baseboards. With a finished attic and basement and a double garage, we had ample space for storage. And the large fenced yard was perfect for Seth's dog. We were within walking distance to the city center, a primary school, a high school, as well as my work and Zeydan's preschool.

Score!

Months later, as Baby nestled in my womb, I nestled in the first place I had ever lived that wasn't an apartment.

Finally. Home!

I was pleased with Seth's motivation to get renovations done in the house before Baby arrived. And despite my being pregnant, I worked with him scraping wallpaper, painting walls, ripping out carpets, changing light fixtures, and tearing up old vinyl flooring. I enjoyed being a homeowner immensely, and I especially enjoyed seeing this new handy and motivated side of Seth. We worked well together, and we grew closer.

Like my rapidly growing belly, my plan for happily ever after was beginning to take shape! Although a minor glitch emerged in my plan when Paul reappeared. He moved back to the area and wanted to start seeing Zeydan again. Zeydan didn't want to see Paul. He didn't understand who Paul was; after all, he had a father figure whom he adored. With some kicking and screaming, Zeydan gradually began seeing Paul until a schedule of every-other-weekend was established.

My pregnancy with Baby was much like that which I had with Zeydan—I was fully mobile and functioning with normalcy and ease. I still had a strong desire for a natural birth, so midwives monitored my pregnancy. To remain in their care, I had to deliver in the hospital, because birthing naturally after cesarean was classified as risky. Considering the naïve and reckless choices I had made with Zeydan's birth, I was happy to follow the advice of the experts this time around.

My estimated delivery date came and went. I tried walking, spicy foods, and sex. But Baby was content in the comfort of my womb, until the day after my midwife did a "stretch and sweep" of my birthing canal.

The hospital birthing room resembled a lovely hotel room. And aside from throwing up from the pain, labour progressed typically and smoothly. I waited patiently while my body and Baby did what they needed to do.

This urge to push, which my midwife kept asking me about, seemed to take forever to arrive. But finally, after hours of waiting and allowing the ebb and flow of my body's natural impulses to take place, the desire to push had arrived. Despite my body's strong impulse to push, I was told to wait while the midwife and her assistant made final preparations. Seth removed himself from the football game and came to my side.

Pushing Baby into the world was hard work. Those animalistic sounds of women giving birth in movies? That was me. As Baby crowned, I reached down to caress Baby's head—the ripened fruit from almost ten months of incubation and hours of arduous labour. My midwife asked that I turn on my side, but at that point, I was too exhausted to give a crap about any potential tearing, so I remained on my back. And with a final push, Baby was brought into the world and placed on my belly. I instantly felt deep rapture with this baby girl—Asia.

The midwives finished the single stitch on my perineal tear, while I cuddled slimly little Asia on my bosom. The suture wasn't a big deal. Everything was kind of numb down there anyway. The bigger deal, however, was the amount of blood on the floor. It looked like a massacre had just taken place, and with the massive amount of bruising between my legs, I appeared to be the survivor of it.

All of that didn't matter to me, though. I was enthralled with Asia. And when Mom brought Zeydan to meet his new sister, I admired my beautiful and whole family. Seeing Zeydan's huge smile and pride at being a big brother was priceless. It made my heart melt. With Seth at my side, and my mom sitting across from me with her faithful and warm smile, I felt like I had finally found my happiness.

The following morning, a photographer came into my hospital room to take photos of me and my new baby, except the photographer took one look at me and walked back out without a word spoken. No offer to take pictures of the baby and me. No offer to come back later.

My confusion as to the why I wasn't offered pictures was remedied when I looked at myself in the mirror—I was not a pretty sight. My face was pasty white and swollen and my eyelids were puffy and nearly swollen shut.

Throughout the day, nurses checked my vitals. My heart rate raced at around two hundred beats per minute, despite my doing nothing other than nurse and lay in bed. Turns out, I had lost sixty percent of my blood during the birth. I needed a blood transfusion.

Note to Self: Good thing you were in the hospital, Girl! Sometimes, the experts do know more than you.

A blood transfusion? This is kind of a big deal. I thought. *Isn't it?* I quickly became petrified as my mind whirled with the what-ifs.

I just wanted to have a baby. I didn't sign up for a blood transfusion! I don't want a blood transfusion!

I needed Seth to assure me that everything was going to be okay. I wanted him to be there to confirm the risks and the facts and to assure me that a blood transfusion was necessary. I wanted him to come and hold my hand while I made the decision.

Seth had been working and was still sleeping when I called. I explained what I felt was big news.

He said okay, hung up the phone, and went back to sleep.

With hesitation and fear, and no support, assurance, or handholding from Seth, I had several bags of blood pumped into my body.

All went well.

What didn't go so well though was my body's recovery from birth. After almost a week in the hospital, I was finally discharged. But the relief of being at home was quickly replaced with excruciating agony. I couldn't pee. All my body could muster after several minutes on the toilet was a few drops or a faint trickle.

After her inspection, the midwife informed me that I had a urinary tract infection. Some potent cranberry juice swiftly cleared up the problem, but my body still wasn't right. From *down there*, oozed a foul-smelling discharge. Not only did this odour fill the entire top floor of the house, but it also seeped to the main floor and greeted those who stepped through the front door.

I could not stand the smell of myself. It was dreadful.

At my four-week postpartum visit with my midwife, I questioned my stench and the massive yet painless lump in my pelvic region. After a brief exam, and without explanation, she promptly referred me to a gynecologist.

Within a couple days, I sat on the gynecologist's table. After his examination of me, I listened to him explain that I was lucky to be alive. A blood vessel in my vaginal wall had burst during the birth, and in its wake was a cesspool of infected blood that slowly leaked from me—the source of the vile and unbearable reek that emanated from my body.

I needed to have the toxic blood removed before my body became septic. Within a matter of hours, I awoke in the recovery room of the hospital. The surgeon had removed a grapefruit-sized pool of rotten blood.

Nice.

I came home late that afternoon with instructions to return to the emergency department in two days to have the six feet of gauze that was jammed inside me removed.

Two days later, on the Saturday of a Thanksgiving weekend, I drove to the hospital while Seth stayed home with the kids. I recited to the nurse the instructions the surgeon had given me. Shortly after, I reclined on the hospital bed, placed my feet in the stirrups, and braced myself while the surgeon on call pulled on the gauze. And pulled. And pulled. And pulled. Until finally, the last of the blood-soaked dressing left my body. I was sent on my way with a napkin to absorb any remaining blood that might "trickle" out.

By the time I got to my car, the entire inside of my pant legs were drenched with blood. I peered behind at the trail I had left and quickly slid into my car, hoping that no one had seen the incident. I returned home. Exhausted. In my blood-soaked car seat.

By the time I got home, my family had already arrived. They insisted that they bring Thanksgiving dinner to me. So, I reclined on the couch to minimize bleeding while Mom swiftly cleaned my car seat. Angelina finalized the meal while the kids played in the basement and the men watched sports on the television in the garage.

Thank goodness for moms and sisters.

The Comfort of Discomfort

With Seth's meager income from being a school crossing guard, he barely had enough money to afford his habits, never mind contribute to the expenses of a home. So, I returned to work when Asia was four months old. Thankfully, my amazing boss let me work from home for several months, so I didn't have to ship Asia off to daycare at such a young age.

Instead of daycare, I sat Asia in a highchair in front of the television and played videos for her to watch while I worked. I thought those *Baby Einstein* videos were doing her good. A year later, I learned that they are slightly brutal for a baby's developing brain.

Ugh.

> *Note to Self:* Oh, let it go, Love. It's okay! Every parent does their best. Don't over-analyze what's good and not good for your kids. Do what you need to do to make it work, as long as the kids are safe, healthy, nurtured, and loved.

Seth persisted with his vision of Plan B and proudly got hired with a construction company. Seth's shifts in this decent-paying job started early in the morning, and I regularly stressed and worried over him being late for work, which he often was. Thankfully, there were no repercussions and he managed to keep his job.

Seth's half-hearted and reckless attitude toward his job was a source of conflict in our relationship because I wanted him to be different. I wanted him to care about what he did. I wanted him to wake up and get to work on time. And when he didn't, I got upset and I sulked like a four-year-old child.

> *Note to Self:* If someone's traits aren't desirable, accept them as they are or end the relationship. Either way, complaining about them and letting them affect your emotional state and sulking about it is of no benefit to anyone.

Again, my hopes for happily ever after began to deaden.

Attached to our house was a garage in which Seth had set up a second-hand wood burning stove along with a television and his video game console. He had removed the front seats from his old car and placed them on the floor in front of the television. Seth began spending most of his time playing video games in the garage. After I cleaned up from dinner and managed the children and their homework, the kids would consistently ask, "Where's Dad?"

To which my answer was always, "In the garage."

Seth and I argued about his man cave. We argued about him being high. We argued about his lackadaisical approach to work, about his lack of helping with chores around the house, about not spending enough time with the family, and about the frequency of sex in the relationship—three times a week was not enough for Seth.

I simply wanted the *Happy Days* Cunningham life. I wanted to be Mrs. Cunningham and see my husband off to work with a packed lunch, a thermos of coffee, and a kiss. Although I refused to marry Seth, I played the role otherwise—I prepared the coffee, made the lunch, and I even kissed Seth farewell at the door.

The thermoses were forgotten at work.

The lunches repeatedly returned home squished.

And eventually, I withheld the kisses out of disappointment and dismay over my squished dream of happiness.

But life continued. Day in and out, I did it all. I worked full-time. Prepared all the meals. Did the laundry. Cleaned the house. Helped with homework. Transported the kids to and from school and did activities with them. And when bedtime finally rolled around, Seth would usually come in to say goodnight to the kids. Regardless though, I could count on him looking to get his sex fix once the kids were in bed. Not only did I not want to have sex because I was exhausted from being the single caregiver and the sole engaged parent in the home, but I was also completely turned off by Seth's uninvolved role in the family and his habits which differed gravely from mine.

Just as my relationship filled with conflict, so too did my body and emotions. I couldn't stand Seth, and I utterly hated my relationship with him. Yet at the same time, I loved him, and I wanted to stay with him.

WTF?

Note to Self: It's okay, Girl. It's normal to feel conflicted! It's called growth. Keep focusing on those inward feelings and listen to them! You've got this!

The conflict persisted, and the arguments escalated. And compounding our many issues, we began to argue over money as well. I was looking to save money, and in the process of creating a budget, I discovered that Seth was withdrawing hundreds of dollars in cash from the bank regularly. He said it was to buy snacks, smokes, coffee, lunch, and the odd lottery ticket. But things weren't adding up for me. Was coffee, take-out, cigarettes, and gambling really costing two hundred dollars a week?

One evening, a budget discussion morphed into an argument over Seth's pot-smoking habit. In an insensitive and demeaning voice, he snapped, "Wake up, Christine. I've been smoking pot every day for almost my whole life."

Reality hit. My heart sank. I had a drug-addict as my partner and a father to my children.

I was blind. I naively thought that Seth smoked pot occasionally, not every day. But as I reflected, I could see the signs were all there. The regular mood swings, the excessive sleep, and the large amounts of empty chip bags, candy wrappers, and cookie boxes that I cleaned up every morning, plus the hundreds of dollars that vanished from the bank account every week. It all made sense now.

Soon we also fought over how I spent my time. After eight years of working at the adult learning center, which had transitioned into a private college, I moved into a similar role at a large healthcare corporation. I was excited about this job that had terrific perks, one of which was weekly noon-hour yoga. I repeatedly read of the benefits of yoga and had wanted to try it for years, so this was the perfect chance. I signed up without hesitation. I also signed up for a Euchre tournament over lunch. Back in our party years, when Seth and I were flirty friends, we shared many great Euchre games. We made a great team.

But when I shared my excitement of these fun things with Seth, he complained and ridiculed me. He degraded me for being selfish and for not coming home on my lunch-hour to have sex with him instead.

It seemed that the more we fought, the more Seth wanted sex. On weekends while the kids and I were eating breakfast on the main floor, Seth would bang on the floor or wall from the upstairs bedroom. This was a regular weekend sound: a brute summoning for me to have sex with Seth. And if I didn't have sex with him before he got out of bed, he would be miserable for the day. So satisfying Seth was something that I just did so he could wake up in a good mood and be a part of the family activities—so I could get a glimpse of happy.

Sticks and Stones

I tried expressing my feelings to Seth about our relationship. We even went to counselling together, but Seth refused to return after the second session. Our discussions around our relationship always ended in heated arguments. He would berate me for my feelings and call me names, and the conversations would usually end with him storming out into the garage.

Name-calling was something that I never grew up with. Yelling and physical abuse? Yes. But verbal abuse and swearing? These were foreign to me. I had never called anyone a name, and I believed that it was psychologically damaging for anyone, especially children, to be called a name.

But it was evident that name-calling was normal for Seth. Berating people and calling them names when they spoke or acted in a way that didn't conform to his wishes was normal to him.

> *Note to Self:* We all do as we learned through our formative years in life. Swearing and name calling is as normal to Seth as having a violent home is normal to you, Christine. It's not bad or wrong. Seth is merely acting in a way that he learned early in life. It's his normal.

Seth favoured Asia over Zeydan, which is natural to some extent I suppose, since Zeydan was his stepson, but the level of favouritism was unreasonable and unhealthy for both kids. If Zeydan was near Asia when she cried, Seth immediately accused Zeydan and pointed blame at him along with disdain and name-calling, like "You're an idiot," or "Stop being so stupid," or simply, "Jerk." When Zeydan got upset as a result and tried to defend himself, Seth frowned upon him further and turned to other disciplinary measures, like taking away Zeydan's games and toys, sending him to his room, slapping him on the face, or yanking the delicate hair at the back of his neck—the same as Seth's dad had done when Seth was a young boy.

And I watched this all unfold. I condoned this treatment of my sweet boy by not taking a firm stance against it. Oh, Seth and I argued over it, but I was too intimidated to stand up for myself, Zeydan, and my values. I was no match for Seth and the anger that would bleed from him during our arguments. I was simply too afraid to face him head on.

And so, I allowed the abuse of my son and myself to continue in my home.

I began bottling up my feelings and withdrawing emotionally. Zeydan did the same—though I was blind to it at the time.

History Repeats Itself

Asia was going on three when I confided to my family of Seth's daily pot habit. I told them of our ongoing relationship issues, how Seth was often high, spending hundreds of dollars a week to fund his habits, spending his time while home in the garage playing video games, and not regularly contributing to the daily responsibilities in the home. They were in shock and clueless as to the life I was living, because I always seemed so happy during our family gatherings. But behind closed doors and beneath the surface, I was despondent.

> *Note to Self:* Consider an acting career, Girl.

With Mom's sympathetic ear, I played out the logistics of splitting from Seth, but the thought of doing that to the kids broke my heart and scared the heck out of me. I wanted a happy family for my kids. I wanted a happy family for me. Mom quietly listened and validated my feelings and concerns. She would have supported any decision I made.

The thought of leaving Seth and all the unknown what-ifs were simply too scary for me. The pain of living with abuse was more comforting and bearable than the fear of separating from it.

I stayed in it.

For the kids.

Just as my mom had done for decades, and surely her mom.

Note to Self: Christine, you are choosing what you know. Even though living in your current environment and conditions is painful and upsetting, it is known to you and is more comforting than the fear of the unknown. It's normal, even though it doesn't feel good.

Mom and I became best friends. We emailed each other every night. Often, I simply shared the menial tasks I had accomplished in the day, while other times I expressed my frustration over my relationship with Seth.

As time passed, life at home became miserable for me. I loved the kids so dearly, but my life with Seth, not so much. In fact, not at all. I took a day off work one afternoon to paint the living room walls. As I painted, Seth harassed me about choosing to paint instead of having sex with him.

I lost it and exploded, "I HATE YOU!" I had no idea what to do with the mix of the uncomfortable feelings that were swirling inside of me. My life had become unbearable, yet I felt trapped and stuck to remain in it.

The fights and arguments escalated. And when Seth and I talked of separating, he said that he would be an "asshole" to me and make my life difficult if we did separate. This heightened my fear at the thought of leaving Seth, and it reassured me that I had made the right decision in resolving to live the status quo and to stifle my feelings.

But I had a strategy. Instead of separating from abuse, I separated from myself—the part of me that felt emotional pain and despair. I shoved those feelings deep down and completely blocked them off. With all the self-help books I was reading, I was able to choose to be the best mom I could be despite the misery of my relationship with their father. I was choosing to make it fun for the kids and not to depend or rely on Seth's mood or his presence for us to feel like a happy family.

> *Note to Self:* Yes, Girl! A shift is happening!
> Hang on tight—it could get bumpy.

Soon enough, children's laughter began echoing in the home. I offered for Seth to join me and the kids, whether it was playing hide and seek, building forts, playing board games, or getting out for bike rides and walks. I stopped responding to Seth's barbaric summoning for sex in the morning, and when he didn't wake up, I simply let him sleep. And when he elected to smoke and play video games instead of being with me and the kids, I accepted it and had fun with the kids regardless.

This is an okay life, I thought to myself. *I can settle. I'm okay without my happily ever after. I can do this… as long as the kids are happy.*

I became proficient at stifling, denying, and ignoring my feelings. I viewed my relationship with Seth as a business partnership—in the business of faking a happy home in which to raise my two children. It was far better than facing my fears and separating and becoming a single parent. Again.

The Body Never Lies

A couple of years of living the status quo had passed. I was happy when it was just the kids and me doing things together, but I rarely smiled, and I was short to temper. There were moments when we had fun together as a family, watching movies, playing *Rock Band*, or going on vacation, but I had low energy and faithfully got severe strep throat infections twice yearly.

One spring, I had a terrible head cold accompanied by a fever. I had a sinus infection in the past, and this felt similar yet slightly different. I wasn't a fan of going to the doctor's office or taking pharmaceuticals, so I managed the discomfort with natural supplements. But then I started experiencing sharp rhythmic stomach cramps—the kind where you have to stop what you're doing and brace yourself, buckle over, and wince until the cramps pass.

Being raised as a hard worker, I plowed on through and continued working and taking care of the kids and responsibilities at home. When Seth came looking for his regular sex fix, I told him I wasn't feeling well. He ridiculed me and accused me of embellishing the pain as an excuse to not have sex with him.

Something wasn't feeling right, though. After several days, I finally palpated the area in my abdomen from which the pain radiated. I discovered a hard and utterly painful lump that was about half the length of an index finger.

Hmm, I thought, *maybe I should get this checked.*

Note to Self: Gee, you think?

I proudly urged Seth to palpate the lump simply to prove and defend myself against his insensitive accusations.

A few days later, I sat in my doctor's office listening to her puzzlingly admit that she had no idea what was going on with my body. She ruled out my appendix and casually sent me away with requisitions for blood work and an ultrasound and a prescription for antibiotics—because when in doubt, take antibiotics, right?

After another few days had passed, I made my way into an ultrasound office across from my work. I watched as the technician passed the wand over my belly. She paused the wand and gasped, "I think it's your appendix." She ran the wand over the painful lump again, "Don't move."

She left the room and returned within a few minutes. With urgency in her voice, she explained, "The radiologist wants to see a live scan." After she meticulously ran the wand over the lump again, she dismissed me, "You can get dressed, but don't go anywhere. If it's your appendix, you'll have to go to emergency and have surgery."

I texted Seth, my mom, and my sister and bewilderingly told them what I had just heard.

The technician came into the waiting area, "Okay. It's your appendix. I've called the emergency department. They're expecting you."

"Um. Okay." Still confused and shocked over what I was hearing. "Wait. Will I have to wait at the hospital? Because the emergency department takes forever."

"No, they're expecting you. You shouldn't have to wait long. You need to go now. This is serious."

Well, I thought to myself as I was leaving, *I need to tell my boss, and Seth is working over an hour away, so he won't be able to pick up the kids from school, so I'll wrap up at work, pick up the kids, and then go to the hospital. I mean, I've been living with this for over two weeks, what's another couple of hours?*

Skeptical of the urgent need for surgery, I left messages with Jasmine, my trusted naturopathic doctor whom I had been seeing since before my pregnancy with Zeydan. Whatever my ailment or that of my children, Jasmine's advice was always spot on and effective. And when she was unsure of a remedy or recommendation, she advised me to see my conventional doctor.

I was afraid to have surgery, and I wanted to hear Jasmine say, "Skip surgery, I have a remedy for that." But alas, I was unable to reach her.

Note to Self: OMG, Girl! Get your ass in the hospital!

I finished my day at the office, picked up the kids from school, and prepared dinner. Arrangements were made for Mom to come later that evening to help care for the children. And when Seth arrived home, we left for the hospital. With mixed feelings covered up with a smile, I pecked Seth on the cheek and kissed and hugged my children goodbye, oblivious to the degree of suffering I was about to endure.

On my way through the sliding doors to the emergency department, my phone rang. Jasmine's name appeared on the display. *Yes!*

I backed out of the hospital to gain better reception while I answered. With tears in my eyes, I explained that I was on my way into the emergency department to be cut open and have a piece of me removed. To my disappointment, I didn't hear the words I so desperately longed to hear.

I sucked up my tears and headed back in.

After the emergency nurses scolded me for not being there hours earlier, they promptly admitted me. I was quickly seen by a skeptical surgeon who reviewed my symptoms and palpated the painful lump. He doubted that it was my appendix, but based on the radiologist's report, he agreed to perform surgery.

After a long night of waiting, it was finally my turn for surgery. Hours later, I awoke in excruciating pain. Once a dose of morphine kicked in, the doctor proceeded to tell me that my appendix had ruptured and stuck to my intestine. I was slowly being poisoned by toxins leeching into my system, and it took him a few hours to clean the mess left in its wake.

Recovery was long and painful. I experienced this interesting thing called referral pain, which I felt as sharp nerve pain in my neck despite the surgery being in my belly. I experienced extreme vertigo in reaction to Codeine to the point where I was hysteric with fear from what I was experiencing. I also couldn't inhale without piercing pain radiating through my chest.

With all these things going on in my body, no position was comfortable. I suffered and remained on my back immobile and incapable of getting out of bed. Eating was out of the equation. I survived solely off fluids that trickled into me though an intravenous line and out of me through a catheter. The surgeon feared I had an internal infection from the toxins, so I was wheeled around from department to department for tests, scans, and ultrasounds.

In the end, I learned that a side effect of abdominal surgery is pockets of air in the abdominal cavity that can migrate and cause great pain, especially when the bubbles linger around the lungs.

That, and that the black stuff to drink for MRIs is disgusting.

My inability to inhale without viciously sharp chest pain made sobbing extremely challenging for me—and sobbing is how I spent each long day and night. I had no hope of ever feeling better. I could not see past the dark and painful reality that my body and my life were in.

I agonized and fought with my body as I tried to catch my breath from sobbing. But each inhale brought with it piercing pain. So, I fought with my emotions as well, but unlike my past, I was not able to chain them and stuff them down. I struggled to breathe and gasped for air as my emotions ran wild. Sounds of a wounded suffocating wild animal escaped from me as I grieved the painful state my body was in. I mourned the toxic life I had subjected myself and my children to. I cried over the death of Daddy and Apu, and I grieved the death of my happily ever after.

My life was at its ultimate low.

For the first time, my grim life had stared me blankly in the face. I saw it as it was. I saw the emotional pain I had suppressed and denied for many years. The pretending I had done. The lies I told myself.

I saw my relationship for what it was. Abuse. For the first time, I had admitted it to myself.

Seth kept working while I was in the hospital, and thus, he rarely visited me. But through it all, Mom faithfully was there, holding my hand. She stayed at the house and looked after the pets, the kids, the cooking, and the cleaning, yet she still found the time to sit at my bedside with a loving, assuring, and sympathetic smile. Sometimes, she would come a second time in the day, bringing the kids with her after they had finished school.

Mom sat soberly by my side and supported me, through my animalistic sobs and all. I saw compassion and understanding in her eyes and felt immense love through her gentle caresses. Aside from the business of the children, few words were spoken between us. The comfort of Mom's loving presence spoke far more than words ever could have in those despairing moments.

Through the love of my children and that from my mom, I slowly gained hope, and with that came strength and a desire to get better.

CHAPTER 3

Blasting Access: Illumining the Path

Doing the best at this moment puts you in the best place for the next moment.

—*Oprah Winfrey*

I was pleased with Seth's willingness to help when I got home from my week-long stay in the hospital. I deluded myself into believing that he had changed as a result of this life-threatening incident. But alas, as soon as I could walk and stand up straight, the relationship reverted to the way it had always been—awful.

When I had the strength to drive, seeing Jasmine was my top priority. Her office was situated in her family's farmhouse on a lush property surrounded by organic vegetable gardens, fruit trees, and flowering bushes. Going to Jasmine's felt like a rejuvenating retreat for my mind, body, and soul. Consultations with her took not only my whole body into consideration, but my entire life, so the hour drive it now took to see her was well worth it.

The moment I stepped onto the wrap-around porch of the large, old farmhouse, I sighed with a feeling of peace and assuredness. I sat in Jasmine's office with my feet snuggled into the sheepskin rug as we dug into what was really going on with me. She alluded that my ruptured appendix was related to issues outside of my body. I sobbed as I confided in her and spoke of the misery I had felt for the past ten years. How I pretended to live a happy life, and how I had not only lied to others about my happiness, but most importantly, to myself.

I left the comfort of Jasmine's oasis armed with homeopathic remedies and instructions for a castor oil pack to dissolve the large lump of scar tissue that had settled beside my belly button from the laparoscopic surgery.

I used my six weeks of short-term leave from work to take care of myself, inside and out. I faithfully followed Jasmine's recommendations, and after a week of daily castor oil treatments, the scar tissue had completely dissolved. Slowly, I regained my strength. I even started to regain some of the massive amounts of hair that I had lost from the trauma and heavy doses of pain medication.

> *Note to Self:* When in doubt, use that
> castor oil pack all day long!

Most importantly, during that period of restoration, I healed my mind and soul. For an hour each day, I engaged in deep personal reflection with crude self-honesty and a willingness to face my greatest fears and to see the lies I had been telling myself. So along with regaining physical strength, I regained emotional, mental, and spiritual strength beyond any level I had yet experienced.

I was ready to make a change—to stand up for myself and end the abuse.

Seth and I had more conversations around separating, but this time he said he was ready to let me go and not be an asshole about it. We maturely talked through the logistics and agreed that Seth would move out. Ironically, the discussions we had around separating were the most mature and meaningful conversations that we had in years, which only made the decision to separate that much more difficult. We still had deep feelings for each other, and we wept as we embraced and assured one another that separating was the best thing for both of us. Unlike the dissolution of my relationships with Nico and Paul, I questioned my decision this time around. I was petrified and worried sick about what was to come, and I still felt a deep connection and love for Seth. But I stayed true to my inner knowing and took the leap. I stepped through my fears and with firm resolution, I decided to split.

Next came the logistics.

We agreed that Seth would move out, and he started looking for a house immediately.

And the kids?

Asia was eight years old, and we agreed that we would tell her together of our decision to separate. We also decided that I alone would tell Zeydan, who was now twelve. And until we told the kids the news, it was to be business as usual.

Our plans to separate became a scary and grim reality that stared me in the face when Seth found and secured a house nearby, but part of me was beginning to feel lighter and more confident about things. With a fast-approaching closing date on Seth's house, the time to tell the kids was imminent.

Asia and I had gone for a trip to the park, and as we walked along the riverbank and adored the ducks wading in the water, Asia said, "It'll be fun with Dad gone. I'll have two houses and two of everything now."

Like a deer caught in headlights, my eyes widened. I managed to keep my mouth from gaping open, and I mustered out, "Oh. What?" I had no idea that Seth had told Asia, nor how much information he had told her, nor when.

It was a sign of things to come.

"When Dad moves out. It'll be good." She continued to explain. "I'll have two houses, and I'll have two Christmases and birthdays. I'll have two of everything."

"Yes. It will be just fine, Honey." And to instill a glimmer of hope and help ease her feelings, I added, "You know… you'll probably get to see Dad more than you do now."

Through the years, Seth spent little quality time with Asia. Her idea of fun was playing dress-up, dancing like a princess, and playing house with her Barbies—things which Seth did not enjoy. So, if he spent time with her, it was watching a movie while he fell asleep (unless it was Transformers or a superhero movie), or it was Asia watching him play video games with Zeydan.

Asia didn't cry after we walked and talked that day, but her emotions found an alternate form of release through an eye infection and vomiting.

Zeydan spent significantly more quality time with Seth than Asia did. Although Zeydan was seeing Paul every-other-weekend, Seth was Zeydan's hero. He called him "Dad." They did man stuff together, things that Paul didn't do, like play video games and drive remote control cars. So, when I told Zeydan that Seth and I were separating, he wailed and sobbed for the loss of the dad that he had adored.

Two months after those dark nights of despair lying lifeless in my hospital bed, Seth moved out. We officially separated.

Initially, Zeydan and Asia both visited Seth at his new house. But after a month had passed, Seth started dating a woman who had children of her own and Seth wanted to build a family with her, and it didn't include Zeydan. I understood that trying to integrate Zeydan into Seth's new family unit would be difficult. But I didn't understand how Seth could shut Zeydan entirely out of his life.

Without warning or explanation, and after ten years of being the dad that Zeydan looked up to, Seth ceased all communication with Zeydan. Zeydan has not spoken with or seen Seth since. I felt deeply saddened for Zeydan as from that point onward, he never received any holiday cards, or even a wish for a *Merry Christmas,* from Seth.

> *Note to Self:* A great time to
> arrange counselling for Zeydan, Girl!

Alienation

With Seth gone, the energy in the home became light and more enjoyable. I enrolled in a local meditation class where I learned the fundamentals of meditation, and that Jesus wouldn't get mad at me for studying Buddha. I started meditating regularly while my fascination and insatiable thirst for spiritual knowledge expanded. Watching Oprah's *Super Soul Sunday* and *Masterclass* became a staple in my life and my favourite thing to do on Friday nights after the kids settled in for bed.

I continued with the commitment I had made earlier to myself when I was in a relationship with Seth—I was going to be present and prioritize quality time with the kids. And so, the kids and I continued with our goofy games, like "Mom-the-monster-under-the-blanket" and the "jumping game" which was simply the kids running and jumping over various heights at which I lifted my legs. We camped together, stayed at random hotels and swam in their pools, biked to the ice cream shop together, tobogganed in the giant snow banks, built snow forts, and went for walks with Cheeko, our Chihuahua, which Seth and the kids had given me for my fortieth birthday.

Note to Self: Nice! You're starting to get the hang of this thing called fun!

Life was beginning to feel breezy.

Until it didn't.

A few months after our separation, Seth became engaged to Mary, the woman he was dating, and she and her children moved into Seth's place. Asia enjoyed regular time with this new and sudden family, and, as anticipated, she was seeing Seth more now than she had when Seth lived with us at home.

Asia enjoyed and embraced this new aspect of her life, and she especially adored Mary's eldest daughter who gave Asia big girl things like purses, fancy clothes, and lipstick. Within six months, Seth and Mary got married. They got a new puppy, a new kitchen, a new hot tub, and a new deck. It was fun and exciting at Seth's house, unlike ours. There was nothing new at our home. Cheeko was getting older and gray. We had Willy, our rabbit, and Zeydan had a pet rat, but new things rarely happened. No excitement. No older sister to admire, just an older brother who mostly disregarded and mocked Asia.

I was mindful, and despite wanting to cry on some occasions, I consistently expressed happiness for Asia and this new side of her dad that she was seeing and enjoying. I was genuinely happy that she was getting meaningful quality time with Seth, but part of me worried about not being a good enough mother in comparison to the new stepmother that had appeared in Asia's life.

Soon, Asia became unusually agitated and confrontational with me.

"Mom, why aren't you giving Dad's ladder back to him? It's his ladder, you know. He carried it home with Grandpa." Asia snapped with disgust and disdain. "You have two ladders now. You should give Dad his ladder back."

Asia no longer called our place "home". Instead, it was the number and street address of our house, and she began calling me "Christine" instead of "Mom." And repeatedly, she'd tell me, "When I'm twelve, I get to decide where I want to live, so if I want to live with Dad, I can."

I had learned to shut my mouth and allow the inner turmoil that arose to settle, rather than question or challenge Asia's comments.

Seth and I began arguing over our time with Asia. We initially agreed to have equal time with Asia, barring Seth's shifts, which were not flexible like my work. Texts from Seth over "his time" with Asia became increasingly saturated with brash and rude words directed at me, including "bitch, stupid, fucking idiot, cow"—to name a few.

I began to wonder if Seth was using Asia as a pawn—attempting to turn her against me to hurt me as I had hurt him—his dream girl who would never marry him or accept him as he was. It became obvious that an effective co-parenting relationship was not feasible.

Despite agreeing to "work things out" with Seth regarding time shared with Asia, I retained a lawyer and hid behind her cold documents that were scripted with harsh legal jargon and blatantly stated facts. It cited Seth's excessive marijuana use, his past lack of involvement as a father, the threatening and abusive texts I was getting from him, and the uncharacteristic behaviours Asia was now displaying in the home.

I purposely avoided Seth's aggression and anger. I wanted as little direct contact with him as possible. I felt safe hiding behind my lawyer.

I followed my lawyer's recommendations and served Seth with an application for full custody and support, for both Zeydan and Asia.

> *Note to Self:* Girl, a simple heads-up would have lessened the blow and the wrath from Seth that followed. But hey, you're doing the best you can, and it's what you feel you need to do. We are all learning. It's okay!

Asia's aggravation with me escalated in the home. "Mom." She snapped. "Why are you trying to change my last name to yours?"

Taken aback, I sincerely questioned, "Why do you think that?"

"Dad told me you wanted to change my last name to only yours."

"Oh, Honey. That's not true. I don't want to do that at all. I think there's some confusion. What I told Dad is that he should be calling me 'your mom,' not 'Christine' when he's talking to you. That's the only thing I said about names. I'm sorry that you're worried about this. Dad really shouldn't be telling you any of this stuff."

Here I was, defending myself against my eight-year-old daughter's inaccurate accusations regarding my court documents. I had previously tried to explain to Seth in person that he should not be calling me "Christine" when he was talking with Asia. To which he barked back, "Well, that's your name, isn't it? Christine Grauer?"

As time passed and court documents flew back and forth between my lawyer, Seth, and the courthouse, Asia continued to become increasingly troubled. One evening when Asia was having a particularly challenging time, she shouted to me from upstairs, "I like Mary better than you." My heart tore into pieces. I questioned the decisions I had made, and my mind began to frantically wonder what I could do or give to Asia to make her like our home more and to make her like me as much as she liked Mary. All I could do was sob.

Zeydan peered out of his door and scolded Asia, "That's not a very nice thing to say to Mom. And Seth is a very bad man."

This was the first time I had heard Zeydan express how he felt about Seth. My home seemed to be crumbling before my eyes. *Oh my gosh.* I thought. *What have I created?*

I think it was a full moon that night.

The next morning, I came around to my senses—I was not going to change a thing about how I parented and raised my children.

With my lawyer in tow, I went to our first case conference at court. The judge sensed Seth's anger and disdain toward me, and he scolded Seth for being outwardly aggressive. The judge stated his recommendation that despite seeing Asia just over forty percent of the time, Seth should pay full support for Asia.

The day following the case conference, Seth reached out to me with a proposal to settle outside of court. Considering the effects the court process was having on Asia, I agreed to Seth's proposal. With my lawyer's assistance, we drew up an overly detailed, final court order. It was settled and done—joint custody with Seth paying child support for Asia at half the guideline amount.

Despite our consented settlement, almost five years of court ensued.

The abusive texts from Seth continued and escalated, "You're such an idiot. You're pathetic. This is going to come back and bite you in the ass. Your greed will cause you to lose your daughter. You're a terrible parent." So, one fine evening, I marched into the police station and filed a harassment complaint as I showed them the texts on my phone. After their visit with Seth, the texts lessened.

I began taking a stand for myself and started to see the things I was willing to tolerate in my life and those I would not.

> *Note to Self:* Yes, Girl! Do not put up with that crap!

Adolescence. Or Is It?

As Zeydan rounded the corner to fifteen, he started withdrawing from routine conversations about school, friends, and life, which I suppose is normal to some degree for teens. But, in place, he had extreme emotional outbursts. One evening he wailed cathartically in the car as we drove back from a visit with family in Toronto, "I don't have a dad. I want a dad." On another occasion, again driving back from Toronto visiting with family, he slammed the car door when we arrived home and sprinted down our street with his arms flailing about while he screamed at the top of his lungs.

All this time, I wanted to be there and have Zeydan confide in me. But he shut down, as he had done long ago.

I didn't see it back then.

In fact, I unknowingly fostered it.

I raised Zeydan to respect me and not to talk back to me. And if he said something that went against my parenting beliefs, I washed his mouth with soap, just like my parents did to me and my sister. I raised him to believe that he had to do things "because I said so" without regard for his opinions or feelings. I raised him to work hard and get stuff done, even if he wasn't feeling well, and that work was more important than play and how he was feeling inside.

Out of desperation, I tried to control his behaviour when it didn't conform to the way I behaved as a child toward my parents. And when my attempts at control didn't work, I'd lose it and scream at him.

I also fostered Zeydan's lack of trust in me because I condoned the physical, emotional, and verbal abuse he received from Seth. I never stood up to it. I expressed my dislike of it to Seth, which always led to fights, but I never protected Zeydan the way this sweet boy deserved to be protected.

> *Note to Self:* Um, yeah! No wonder Zeydan was closed off as a teenager. Just know that you did the best you could, given your own issues and story, Girl! Trust that each soul chooses their journey—parents, problems, and all.

Some Relief

Life at home became more fun for the kids and me when Roger became an integral part of our lives. I met Roger, a tall, muscular, and fair-haired man, through online dating. Aside from being handsome, he was responsible, and he reliably did the mundane daily chores in life, the things which Seth rarely did. Roger was well-educated, healthy, fit, generous, and kind, and he had a professional career as an engineer. I instantly liked him, and after a few months of dating, I introduced him to the kids.

Since Roger was manly and liked to fish and hunt and eat lots of meat, Zeydan instantly liked him and bonded with him. I finally met a man who was not only kind, educated, generous, and good-looking, but in the same breath he could change light fixtures, repair plumbing, and install new flooring with precision and care. He met all my needs at the time, and I became smitten with him.

Together with the kids, we'd have regular dinners after which, we'd thoroughly enjoy our time rock-climbing. Roger always helped do odd jobs around the house, and he'd even show up unannounced to shovel the driveway or mow the lawn. Together with my kids, we went on vacations to his family's cottage and we portaged through the wild backcountry of Algonquin Park.

I was so pleasantly surprised by this kind and capable man, who was well articulated. *And* he did domestic work around the house. *And* he didn't hit or berate me or smoke up. It was like a dream come true. It was the start of my happily ever after. Finally!

Except...

Roger's two teen daughters rejected my kids and me. So, Roger lived a separate life with his daughters that detracted from our time together. Not ideal, but the amount of companionship and fun we had when we were together made up for the times we were apart. But that sense of separateness always lingered in each of our minds.

I decided to take the kids to Germany to meet their large, extended family for the first time. When I was in high school and university, Angelina and I went every-other-year to visit with our family abroad. Although it had been over fifteen years since my last visit, I had a connection with my relatives and kept in contact with them over the years.

Our first stop was Wales, the United Kingdom, where we visited with a friend for a few days. We admired and reveled in this strange and foreign land with its lush, green rolling hills littered with grazing sheep, its tight and winding roads on which we drove on the wrong side, and the old cobblestone streets in the towns with pubs that surprisingly welcomed children. At the end of our stay, the kids and I ventured on our own to see the sights of bustling London, England, before we continued our adventure.

Next stop: Germany, near Stuttgart, to visit with my mom's side of the family. My uncle and aunt had a large home with a separate apartment on each of their four floors. They resided on the top floor, while two of my cousins and their families lived on the other levels. The modern yet cozy basement apartment was vacant, and this is where we stayed.

For over a week, we enjoyed being an integral part of the lives of my aunt and uncle and my four cousins and their large families. Together, we ate traditional German meals, played games, sang, hiked, went sight-seeing, and visited with more of my aunts and their families.

We were in tears saying goodbye to my mom's side of the family as we were welcomed into my dad's side. Closer to Frankfurt, we stayed in my uncle's home, which also had four separate apartments. Here, we spent most of our time with my cousin and her two teenage daughters doing much of the same activities that we had done with my mom's family. We also went to visit my dad's gravesite. I wished I could have reminisced and told stories about my dad, but with no conscious memory of him, we simply admired the beautiful grounds and the fresh and sunny spring day.

My uncle, a spitting image of my dad, filled in the gaps about my dad as he told stories while he barbequed and poured beers for the large family gatherings. Zeydan delighted in the abundance of food and beer, while Asia delighted in hanging out with her older cousin, to whom she related as a big sister.

After two weeks in Germany, we began our voyage home, but not without taking advantage of our flight's layover in Reykjavik, Iceland. Here, we were in awe of the lava-crusted landscape and dim nights, which never exposed the black of night to which we were so accustomed at home. We stayed in a finely-furnished hotel in a room supplied with two beds, a bathroom, and a small kitchen. During our three-day stay, we soaked in the steaming sulfur waters of the Blue Lagoon, toured the landscape, and learned the fascinating history of the land and culture.

To my surprise, the kids weren't as happy to arrive back home as I was. Instantly they asked when they could return to see their family abroad. Zeydan expressed his desire to return and trek the country of Iceland on his own. But, as amazing as our trip was, it was a source of stress for Zeydan back at school. He had always excelled in school and found it easy, but in grade nine, work had piled up during his almost three-week absence. I was remiss in not being more involved in the work his teachers had assigned to him for our vacation.

Little did I know this stress was the rock that started an avalanche of one of the toughest trials of my life.

Emotional Shock

Shortly after our return from Germany, I received a text from Paul—he was arrested and being investigated for a privacy crime at the wellness clinic in which he was working. He wanted to tell Zeydan of the news personally before Zeydan learned of it from the press or friends.

In shock, I handed Zeydan the phone and gave him privacy. Moments later, wails, screams, and pounding on the floor and walls echoed through our home. Asia and I stared at each other with shock and alarm. I explained to her what had happened, although I was unable to explain the *why* behind it.

After Zeydan quieted down, we spoke of what had happened. He was confused and distraught over the news he had just heard. I was equally confused and felt helpless in being able to provide him with the answers he sought and the comfort he needed. Instead, I urged him to keep up with his responsibilities and go to Boy Scouts that night. I was barely equipped to handle my own feelings, let alone my son's. So,

I urged him to do what I had always done, press on through and just keep working.

> *Note to Self:* Yeah. A night off to process feelings would
> have done Zeydan some good, as well as talking
> to a professional. But what's done is done,
> and it's all for a reason, Christine.

Within a matter of months, life at home became tense and stressful. I tried using access to WiFi at home as leverage, and, well, bribery, to get Zeydan to go to school, but he kept skipping classes—a lot. He began outwardly refusing to heed my requests to not have so many friends over during the day. He started not only talking back to me but telling me to fuck off. On one afternoon, after he learned that I had told his friend's mom that her son was at our house and so high that he was barely functioning, Zeydan entered my bedroom, stood next to me, and bellowed down at me, "Snitches get stitches."

I made frequent calls to the principal and social worker at Zeydan's school. I called Paul to ask for his advice. I called Paul's dad, whom Zeydan was close with, and asked him to come and talk to Zeydan. I finally stopped trying to control Zeydan's behaviour and instead approached him from a caring and concerned perspective trying to get to his *why*—but to no avail, he remained closed. I was beginning to run out of options to help support my adult-sized teen son, who was becoming more and more antagonistic in the home.

Aggression had returned in my life. This time from my own son.

I continually tried to talk with him to understand what he was experiencing, and when incidents escalated in the home, I suggested that Zeydan stay at his dad's if he wasn't happy at home with me. When he took the Wi-Fi box and hid it, as I discovered one morning while attempting to work from home, I reached my limit of tolerance. I warned Zeydan that soon it wouldn't be a choice to stay at his dad's.

The hostility continued. Not only did I have my comfort to think about, but Asia's as well. And at this point, Asia didn't like going to Seth's house, because Seth and Mary were frequently fighting. I wanted to provide Asia with a safe and stable home, which she could always find comfort in. And with Zeydan lashing out, home did not feel so safe and comforting.

After exhausting my resources, I decided it was time for Zeydan to live at Paul's. On a Saturday when Zeydan was at Paul's, I dropped off a large duffle bag of his clothes and told him that he was going to be living there for a while.

The backlash from Zeydan was nothing I could have ever prepared for. I received text after text of being called every foul name possible. I was told he never wanted to see me or talk to me again—this was goodbye forever.

No pain I had experienced to this point in my life could compare to the anguish and distress I felt from hearing such cold words from my son. My beloved first-born who snuggled next to me as a baby while he sucked his thumb and rubbed my eyebrow with his pinky finger. My son with whom I'd shared endless hours walking and playing at the park, shopping at the malls and grocery stores, playing with cars and molding clay, reading stories before bed, watching Barney on TV, and visiting friends and family. My son whom I loved so dearly and would die for.

I spent most of the next three days in bed bawling. I was immobile from heartbreak and emotional anguish. Roger was kind and tried to help. He wanted to take me out to get my mind off things, but I simply couldn't stop crying, whether in public or not.

After the third day of isolating myself and barely eating, I went to a hot yoga class. During class, I felt a veil of heavy emotional energy lift from me. It was palpable, and what remained was an unexpected feeling of peace. I left the class feeling resolved and stable.

It would be a month until I saw Zeydan next.

Note to Self: Hold little weight in the things that people utter in the heat of the moment.

Stirring of Something Greater

I met my dear spiritual mentor at a local spiritual conference. He had travelled from New York to present at this conference, and there was something about him that I immediately connected with. We exchanged some heartfelt words in our small introductory breakout group, and while waiting in line at the coffee break, he stood beside me and smiled at me. He glanced above my head, as if to see something, and said that I was doing just fine and that everything was going to be okay. It wasn't until he presented his talk on the power of "I AM" that I realized his name was George—the same name that had come to me repeatedly during my meditations for years prior.

From that moment, George was my trusted mentor who guided me on my spiritual journey in this thing called life. We exchanged emails and texts, and I talked with him on the phone. I saw him twice yearly in the Catskill Mountains in New York during spiritual retreats. The energy I felt surging through my body during my teachings with him was unlike anything I'd ever experienced. Something tremendous and magnificent was stirring within me and beginning to come to the surface.

Shortly after meeting George, I began reading a book from Wayne Dyer, and in it, I learned of a woman whose life's work involved referencing self-help books and talking to people about it—and from this, she earned decent income. She was a life coach.

Gosh, I thought, *A life coach? I want to do that!*

I mean, I liked my job and the people with whom I worked, but at this point, I was consuming personal growth and spiritual books like mad and had been doing so for almost twenty years. I had an insatiable thirst for deep knowledge that presented a different way of being and a different way of living than that to which I, and the rest of society, had become accustomed. I knew there was another way to live. I knew there was more going on in life than what I was taught, and I was hot on the trail of figuring it out.

I did some digging, and before I knew it, I was attending an online training session with Holistic Learning Centers in the United States. After the two-hour introductory class, I was hooked. Without hesitation, I signed up for my Spiritual Life Coach Certification.

I had no idea what I was getting myself into.

The program was demanding and intense—only three of the ten people from my class graduated and attained their certification. It was like a second full-time job. I was required to do hours upon hours of homework, apply the exercises and practices on myself, attend two-hour weekly classes, complete a practicum, and undertake a great degree of deep and intensely personal introspection.

While I was learning things like mature boundary protection, I conveniently had my life in which I could apply and practice the principles and techniques I was studying. I was learning to assert my boundaries in an emotionally mature way (without screaming things I'd later regret). I was learning to provide myself with the unconditional love and nurturing that I had always sought from others. I was learning to detach from people with whom I was entangled and whose energy and actions were affecting me in unhealthy ways. I was learning to create a life where I felt more happiness and love.

With this new knowledge and ability, George's guidance, and my life coach's constant support, I unraveled a new me. I now had a deep sense of who I truly was. I was beginning to sense, develop, and trust my intuition. Feelings of peace and contentment began to saturate my days. I had an inner knowing and confidence that nothing could alter this strong foundation that I was unearthing from within. And life continually provided the classroom in which I could apply, practice, and integrate this new way of being.

I was no longer emotionally triggered by Seth's attempts at alienating Asia from me. I knew so clearly who I was and who I wanted to be for my children. I could tell when my protective personality (ego) was stepping in and trying to take control versus my Higher Self (the real Me). I had a strong knowing and deep trust in the process of life, and that all things, including the seemingly bad, were a necessary part of unraveling the perfection of life.

Turn of the Tide

Asia began confiding in me about how she didn't like being at Seth's. He was shunning his fatherly responsibilities and wasn't spending time with her. At ten years old, she was solely responsible to wake herself up, make herself breakfast, and get ready for school. And when it was time for her to wake up Seth to drive her to school, she feared doing so because he was usually grouchy and foul from her waking him. Asia complained to me that the frequent fights between Seth and Mary were intense, and to avoid them, Asia spent most of her time in her dim room.

I supported. I allowed.

With my growing sense of my Inner Self, I provided a solid foundation for Asia at home, and I sympathized with her as she continued to express her feelings about her relationship with Seth. Seth and Mary split, and Asia was excited to find a new place with Seth and build a new relationship and a new home together with him. But as one might guess and despite the new environment and fresh start, Seth soon slipped into his old patterns and behaviours of which I was so familiar. Asia complained of Seth's lack of parenting and responsibility in the home and how she played the role of the responsible mother of the home, which was a source of conflict between her and Seth.

Asia found marijuana in a small bag on the floor of Seth's bedroom, and when she asked him about it, he barked back that he was smoking it almost his whole life—not the response a pre-teen is hoping to hear from her parent.

Soon, Asia hated going to Seth's. While there, she faithfully texted me that she didn't want to be there and that she wished she was at home with me. I empathized with her and sent lots of cute and loving emojis. We'd stay connected for hours as I helped her with homework over text, or we'd sneak in a phone or video call together, while Seth was in the shower or outside smoking. She started skipping nights at Seth's place to stay with me or to sleepover at friends' homes. Asia was content with staying at Seth's as little as possible, and Seth didn't object either—until I requested that he recommence paying child support, which I had previously waived in good faith when he and Mary split.

Naturally, Seth lashed back with endless texts of vulgar accusations and threats. To which I responded that I would reinstate the former court order for support to be deducted directly from his pay and that I was blocking his number from my phone. His number remains blocked to this day.

> *Note to Self:* Yes! You go, Girl!
> Way to assert yourself and set boundaries!

Hours following my request for Seth to recommence child support payments, Asia received repeated texts from Seth—he relentlessly questioned why she wasn't at his place more often. And then, after several back-and-forth texts, and for the first time in her life, Asia texted Seth exactly how she felt. But, despite her emotional honesty and courage in finally telling Seth the truth of her feelings, he belittled her feelings, denied what she had written, and defended himself.

Asia's time at Seth's continued to dwindle until it ceased altogether when she was twelve. Thankfully, I was home that final day. I answered the door wondering who was ringing the bell so early on a Sunday. And there, to my complete surprise, stood Asia with tears streaming down her face. I quickly welcomed her in and embraced her while she wept hysterically.

As I peered out the door in confusion, Seth yelled from the open window of his car, "You won, Christine! You won!" And he squealed out of the driveway.

Once Asia could breathe normally between sobs, she explained that Seth insisted that she go to a walk-in medical clinic that morning because she had a stuffy nose. After standing her ground and refusing to go, Seth snatched her cellphone from her hands and left her room with it. Asia was worried that Seth was reading messages between her and me that expressed how desperately she wanted to come home rather than be at Seth's place. She was terrified about how he'd react. Moments later, Seth returned to Asia's room. He tossed the phone at her and told her to pack her shit because he was taking her to her mother's.

When It Rains

I had managed to establish some base communication with Zeydan while he was living at Paul's. A month into his stay there, I arranged to pick him up to get his health card renewed. I was thrilled that he was willing to see me, especially after the texts I had received from him, saying he never wanted to see me again.

Our talk on the drive to the government health office was a good one. Zeydan spoke with maturity and respect. He said he learned a lot in the past month about not only himself but also about the local bus system since he had to take the bus to school for a couple of weeks. He said he didn't like being at Paul's and wanted to come home.

"Sure, after you attend counselling," was my reply.

Note to Self: Uh oh. I've heard this conditional agreement before. But it's totally understandable, Christine. He's your son, and you want to have him back home.

I connected with a counsellor, and Zeydan willingly attended. At this point, he was willing to jump through hoops to come back home. His homework for the next session was to list chores he could do around the house, along with behavioural expectations and consequences.

Zeydan had his list done within an hour of that first appointment. I was proud and impressed at Zeydan's proactive participation and his reasonable and wise suggestions.

We attended the next counselling appointment together, during which we worked through the list that Zeydan had drafted. It also described my unacceptable actions and consequences, like if I yelled at Zeydan, I would have to do one of his chores that week. Zeydan was also expected to see a psychologist bi-weekly, and he added that I was required to see a psychologist as well.

Through a collaborative effort, we arrived at an informal contract, which we both signed at the third and final appointment with the counsellor.

Note to Self: Someone living in your house under strict rules is more like the military than a home. It's not a means to foster trust and love in a relationship—in fact, it promotes rebellion and doubt. You're doing okay given what you know, Love!

With a signed contract in hand, Zeydan returned home just in time for his summer school course.

Month one at home was excellent. All went smoothly and according to the contract. I commended Zeydan on his great effort and how well I thought things were going in the home. I suggested that we forget the contract and added that if we could simply respect and communicate openly with one another, things would continue to go well.

Month two at home? Not so great.

With the absence of structure and routine that summer school provided the month prior, Zeydan began hanging out with friends more and more. He stayed out overnight despite my requests to come home. I wouldn't know where he was nor whether he was coming back. While he was out, he generally didn't respond to my texts. And when he did reply to my questions of his whereabouts or plans, it was confrontational and disrespectful.

The contract? I tried bringing it into discussions. Zeydan simply crumpled it into a ball and threw it at me while telling me to fuck off.

Fall approached, and with it, Zeydan started grade ten. Within a month or two, Zeydan began skipping classes again, and the aggression and defiance in the home escalated. I spoke with Zeydan's psychologist, his teachers, school counsellors, and the vice principal to get a handle on what was happening. Everyone was supportive, accommodating, eager, and prepared to help us in any way they could.

It felt like I was living with Seth again. When I tried to enforce rules and stand my ground in the home, I'd hear "bitch" and "fuck you" in response. It felt like I had lost control over the environment in my home.

One weekend, I found a bag of marijuana in Zeydan's backpack—actually, Cheeko sniffed it out (I'm pretty sure he was a police dog in a past life). I took the bag of weed without telling Zeydan and flushed the contents down the toilet.

Can you say *tipping point*?

I had always set my purse and work bag on the stairs near the door the night before work to help me get out of the house swiftly in the mornings. On this particular Monday morning, I had a hunch to check my purse before heading out the door for work to ensure the ten dollars was still in my wallet. Not only was the money gone, but the wallet was gone as well.

I stormed up to Zeydan's room, furious and determined to wake him up. After screaming at Zeydan to wake up and give me my wallet, I yanked at the sheets to which he clung so tightly that he almost fell off the bed along with the sheets.

> *Note to Self:* Not a proud moment, Momma. Next time try deep belly breathing first to calm your emotional reactivity before engaging with others in a triggered and potentially harmful state. But I still love you and I forgive you.

I screamed, "You have ten minutes to return my wallet. If you don't return it, I'm calling the police."

The last time I said I would call the police was when Zeydan was uttering crude names at me. But the police wouldn't come to talk to a teen who was merely telling his mom off—they would only appear if there was harm being done to a person or property, so to Zeydan my threat was empty.

Believing this was simply another bluff, Zeydan hopped in the shower and got ready for school. I grabbed his cell phone and held on to it to ensure he remained home until the police arrived. And this time, they did—precisely as Zeydan walked past the door asking me for his cell phone and mocking me that I was bluffing.

The police officers played good cop/bad cop and said some cold and harsh things to Zeydan. The bad cop raised his voice and threatened to apprehend Zeydan if he didn't give the wallet back. What unfolded next broke my heart. Before me stood my sixteen-year-old son in a man's body. Yet, all I could see was a scared boy who had endured emotional shock and confusion from his dad's criminal actions. A boy who had experienced abuse and abandonment from his beloved stepdad of ten years. And a boy who couldn't confide with his mother because she had cared more about conformity and contracts than feelings.

The police barricaded the doorway as Zeydan tried to escape while screaming, "I just want to go to school like a good boy."

I stood and watched as I held back my tears.

Zeydan relented and slowly made his way up the stairs to his room. He returned the wallet and left for school.

Utterly shaken, distressed, and emotionally unstable, I worked the remainder of the day from home.

The following Wednesday morning, I worked in the dining room while Asia got ready for school upstairs in her bedroom.

As I worked at the table, Zeydan approached me and demanded, "Give me seventy dollars or give me the weed."

A calm, "No," was my reply.

"What's it going to be… seventy dollars or the weed?" He demanded.

"Oh, I'll give you the weed. When you're nineteen."

Zeydan calmly walked away and sat on the couch in the living room, which was adjacent to the dining room.

The profanity began.

I asked Zeydan to stop, but the profanity continued and his anger grew. He threw a glass across the room. Surprisingly, it didn't shatter (shout out to IKEA), but it was enough to scare me and question what might follow next. It was like Zeydan became possessed with rage. I told him I would call the police if things continued.

I don't recall the stream of aggressive and mocking words that flowed from Zeydan's mouth, but the rage rising in the room was palpable and unforgettable. In one swift motion, he stood up and flipped the solid oak/iron/slate coffee table in the living room along with the items stored under it and resting on its surface.

With Zeydan yelling profanities in the background, I called police dispatch and reported the situation. They took the call seriously as there was physical aggression, property damage, and a minor in the home. In a matter of minutes, the police arrived, but not before Zeydan left for school. The police interviewed Asia and me, and because Asia was a minor, they reported the incident to Family and Children's Services.

Echoes of being told to fuck off and the crash of the coffee table smashing into the floor played over and over in my mind. I fretted and felt helpless, as I came to the painful realization that my son would have to leave home again—this time for longer than the last.

When Zeydan returned home, few words were spoken. The air was cold and tense.

Despite my urging Zeydan to be home for the appointment with Family and Children's Services, he didn't attend. Since Asia did not want to be at Seth's, the only solution to appease the worker was for Zeydan to leave. Later that night, I explained the outcome of the meeting to Zeydan. He could not understand why he had to go and not Asia. I explained that Asia leaving was not an option, considering she was younger and did not want to be at Seth's. Zeydan did not want to return to Paul's, so a couple of weeks later Zeydan began living with his grandparents, about two hours from Waterloo.

As I hugged my sweet son goodbye, I questioned the choices and decisions I had made. My heart tore into pieces asking Zeydan to leave home again, but I felt a tiny bit of solace knowing that his grandparents adored Zeydan, and that he enjoyed spending time with them.

Family and Children's Services closed their file.

The next time I would see Zeydan was to visit him in the hospital eight months later.

Change Is the Only Constant

After Asia had lived with me full-time for six months, I emailed Seth and requested that he pay the full amount of child support, since he had only been paying half. In a matter of hours, I received texts from Asia while she was at her friend's house. She was terrified and asked me to help her because Seth was repeatedly texting her and threatening to call the police on her because she wasn't going to his place like the court order stipulated. I assured her that the police wouldn't take her away kicking and screaming like they would a two-year-old child.

After Seth's backlash and his refusal to pay the guideline amount of support, I served him with court documents. Again. This time though, I chose to be my own lawyer because no lawyer could convey the fear and worry that I heard in Asia's voice when she explained the things she had experienced at Seth's. And when I'd represented myself in the past, the judges listened, unlike the times that lawyers had spoken on my behalf. No one knew my story like I did, and the compassion and authenticity in stating my case struck a human cord in the process-laden court system. So, I prepared all my documents, did all the court filing, and selectively consulted a lawyer to ensure I was interpreting the legal requirements accurately.

I was so engrossed with working at my job, managing Asia's school and extracurricular activities, managing the house and chores, managing the rental townhome that I had just purchased, taking courses for my life coach certification, and being a part-time lawyer that I didn't have time to think about my happily ever after—it was placed on pause.

With just Asia, Cheeko, and me at home, things were quiet, but we got into a groove, and our mother-daughter relationship flourished. I supported Asia as she endured extremely tough times in middle-school, where kids mocked and ridiculed her for her slim and tall body (because "thick" was in), and where her best friend betrayed and bullied her. Asia dreaded and resisted going to school because of the social torment. On one occasion, she called me in tears hiding in a bathroom stall. She asked me to come and get her because her ex-best friend was being mean and it was upsetting her. My response was (painfully) "No." I told Asia that she was strong enough to stand up for herself and to refuse to accept that kind of treatment any longer. Thankfully, it worked, and Asia learned to defend herself.

> *Note to Self:* Phew. Good job, Momma. As parents, we
> want to step in and protect our children, but at some
> point, the little birds need to fly on their own.

Asia frequently told me that I was her best friend. With her catty friends at school, Asia and I spent a lot of time together. We shopped, walked, visited with family, read, and did mindful breathing. I dropped her off and picked her up from school. I watched and supported her while she did gymnastics. And I helped her with homework. Regular mom stuff. And when time allowed, we spent time with Roger. We also did simple renovations around the house together which was Asia's favourite pastime.

As much as the two of us were in a groove, we missed Zeydan immensely, and we worried about him. Asia, Roger, and I went to see George for the semi-annual spiritual retreat in the Catskill Mountains, and during the retreat, Asia and I explained to George the things that were happening with Zeydan. With George's love and guidance, we experienced a beautiful moment of healing within the compassionate and genuine group of like-hearted souls we were among. It gave us hope.

I continued to text Zeydan and let him know what was happening at home. I told him that he was loved and missed and that I thought of him often. I rarely got responses, and I became okay with that. I expected that Zeydan was feeling a mix of confusion and painful emotions. I simply gave space and allowed.

In the New Year, Zeydan and Paul reunited and moved in together in a two-bedroom apartment in Waterloo. Zeydan began taking courses at school again during the new semester—it was an opportunity for a fresh start for him, and we were all hopeful. Occasionally, I'd drive past Zeydan as he walked to or from school, and I'd wave in passing. In return, I'd get the middle finger.

Soon after starting school, Zeydan stopped attending. He spent his days alone in the apartment, while Paul worked from sun-up to sun-down at his job.

As winter turned to spring and spring turned to summer, I started getting more conversational texts from Zeydan. We corresponded about life, my past, my relationship with Seth, and my aversion to weed. We got into some deep conversations about spirituality. I believe Zeydan had some intense spiritual experiences while under the influence of weed, and he was encouraging me to also get high, so I could experience the same.

I was happy that Zeydan was reaching out to me, and on one night, Zeydan also reached out to Roger, Mom, and Asia, but his texts were alarming and incoherent. To my mom, Zeydan asked for help, saying that I was trying to abuse him sexually. To Asia, he sent two pictures—the first one was of his face fully masked with cloths with only a narrow slit through which his eyes peered through, and the second was of his apartment walls covered with dozens of taped X's covering every crack and hole in which he thought Paul had hidden micro-cameras. To Roger, he said that I was dying, and that Roger should go help me.

I called Paul and relayed the flurry of messages we were receiving, and I urged him to check on Zeydan.

The next morning, I learned from Paul that he couldn't enter the apartment the night prior because Zeydan had chained the door and barricaded it with the couch. Paul went to the police for assistance.

A few days later, I heard my son's voice for the first time in about eight months. With disbelief and delight, I tripped up the stairs and bolted into Asia's room to share the message with her.

With tears in my eyes, I stared at her, "Zeydan wants to come home."

I played the voice message on speakerphone, "Umm… hi, Mom. It's your son, Zeydan. I'm in the hospital, and I'm in a bit of a bind. I was wondering if it would be okay to come home."

Asia stared at me, and with excitement and hesitation said, "I don't know if I'm ready."

"I don't know either, Honey. But this is great! We'll go slow. I'll go by myself and talk to him first."

Aside from Roger and the staff in the youth mental health center at the hospital, I was the only person Zeydan wanted to see. And there, in a private room with cameras monitored by staff, my sweet son hunched down, hugged me, and wept inconsolably as we embraced.

We sat together and talked for over an hour. I tried to make sense of the things Zeydan was saying about a girl, a friend, a broken heart, and betrayal. About the staff in the hospital who were conspiring against him. And about people who were trying to harm him. I tried to understand his stories, and not discredit them. Anything is possible, right?

As much as I tried and wanted to deny it, it was clear that Zeydan was experiencing things that were not happening in my reality. I wanted it all to be a dream. I wanted to believe so desperately that none of this was happening and that we could just go back to the way things used to be—when we played and romped and had fun together.

Instead of participating in the programming at the center, Zeydan sat in his room for hours facing a wall. And as long as he refused to participate in activities, he could not be released from hospital care.

I saw Zeydan every day, and Roger visited occasionally as well. Once Zeydan was granted day passes, Asia joined me, and we took Zeydan to the hospital cafeteria for dinners.

There, we played games together and became reacquainted as a family.

While in Zeydan's room one day, a psychiatrist entered and explained that marijuana affects different people in different ways and that for Zeydan, marijuana affected his brain and that he should stay away from it. Zeydan could not see any problems, other than him being locked in the hospital with these people who were conspiring against him.

Daily, with frustration and confusion in his voice, Zeydan asked me why he was locked in a hospital and how he got to be there. He questioned why, as his mother, I simply couldn't sign him out—to which I explained that his participation in the activities was his ticket out. And every night when I retired to the privacy of my room, I'd cry muffled sobs into my pillow. My heart ached to see my son endure such suffering and confusion.

Surely, no person should ever have to experience this.

Eventually, Zeydan committed to select activities in the program, and gradually, he participated and earned an off-site day pass. The following day, Zeydan was granted an overnight pass. We welcomed him home with a barbeque dinner and a celebratory cake. He settled in nicely, as though he had never been gone. It felt good and right to have my son back home. It brought relief and happiness, sprinkled with a dash of uncertainty as to what our new lives together would look like.

After two weeks in the hospital, with paperwork in one hand and medication in the other, Zeydan was formally discharged from the hospital.

My son came home.

The Police, a Mental Health Nurse, and the Culligan Man

Zeydan and I had some deep and meaningful conversations during his first weeks at home. He told me personal things about his soulmate and his friend, and he shared in his feelings about them. He also told me how he could communicate with deceased people, including my dad.

I was so thankful that my son finally felt he could confide in me, and I listened with an open mind and an open heart. I couldn't relate to many of the things he was telling me, but I honoured his truth and I empathized with him, providing suggestions when I felt there was room for them. I remained mindfully present during those moments. I actively listened and asked meaningful questions.

Zeydan proudly accomplished the list of chores he had around the home. It was a pleasure having him back. He had a quirky sense of humor that I enjoyed, and I could always count on him to provide open and honest opinions on things. He also had a hearty appetite, and I appreciated that my cooking was well received. I also relished in hearing the beautiful music coming from the basement, as he adeptly strummed his guitar day after day. Those were the moments where I stopped what I was doing and became fully present. I felt the harmony in the air and absorbed it into my being along with the joy that I felt for having my son back home.

Soon after returning home, though, Zeydan refused to take his medication. The agreement he had drafted and signed in the hospital went into the garbage.

My happily ever after remained on pause. Again.

Asserting boundaries and limits with my son, who was antagonistic and suspicious, while trying to keep the home peaceful for Asia's comfort, proved to be challenging (to state it mildly). And to add to my efforts, I was concurrently playing part-time lawyer and helping Asia have her voice heard, respected, and acknowledged with her dad and the court system. Not to mention that I was working full-time while simultaneously completing my life coaching certification.

My goal was to maintain an environment in the home where everyone could feel comfortable and safe. Both children refused to see their dads for their own valid reasons, and

Zeydan now also refused to see his grandparents. Zeydan and Asia had nowhere to go if the going got rough at home, so the pressure was on for me to maintain balance and safety in the home.

I refined my definition of "important," and I carefully chose my battles. I allowed Zeydan to do as he pleased in the home, except for select boundaries on which I was firm. And when I asserted those boundaries, anger would surface in Zeydan, and he'd revert to crude name-calling and banging walls and doors in the house. So, I carefully chose to uphold my boundaries at times when Asia wasn't home.

I received my first call from the police while I was at work. I was expecting it to be the Culligan Man—the people who sell and service water softeners because the water in the Waterloo region is hardened with minerals that destroys the plumbing. But instead of the Culligan Man, it was the police. The officer said he received a complaint and needed to speak with Zeydan.

I quickly left work to let in the police officer who was waiting at my house. I awoke Zeydan with a knock on his bedroom door and told him that the police wanted to speak with him. After confirming that the police officer wouldn't leave (as Zeydan had requested), the officer entered Zeydan's bedroom. He explained that they had complaints from girls who had received excessive and harassing texts from Zeydan.

I peered into the bedroom from the doorway and listened as the police officer flipped open his little black notebook and read to Zeydan some of the texts the girls had reported, "I'm a little concerned over these texts, Zeydan. What's going on here? These texts don't make sense, and I'm worried about them and you."

Their twenty-minute dialogue ended with Zeydan having an emotional release and agreeing with the police officer to speak with a nurse who made house-calls. As the officer began to leave Zeydan's room, I darted downstairs. Still expecting the Culligan Man and now the nurse, I quickly placed a note outside the door of my front porch, informing my expected guests that the doorbell was broken and to enter the house without ringing the bell.

The mental health nurse on wheels arrived within minutes. Along with the police officer, we gathered in the kitchen while we waited for Zeydan. I explained that Zeydan had recently been discharged from the youth mental health unit at the hospital after his agonizing two-week stay, and that he was no longer taking medication.

Zeydan soon joined us in the kitchen, and he proceeded to fry himself eggs while he chatted with our house guests.

As timing would have it, I peered down the hallway, and there stood the Culligan Man stopped dead in his tracks with his mouth agape and his eyes staring blankly at the group of us in the kitchen—myself, the mental health nurse, the police officer, and Zeydan standing over crackling eggs.

In full amusement over what was unfolding in my house, I raised my arm high and waved. With a grin, I blurted, "Welcome to the party!"

I escorted the Culligan Man to the basement to deal with the fussy water softener. As I directed him to the softener, I jovially asked if the scene into which he had just entered would make dinner table conversation that evening.

Obviously still stunned, he apologized for my seeming predicament, put his head down, and inspected the water softener.

After the crowd left and the excitement settled, the status quo resumed in the home as though what had just taken place was merely a faint memory from years ago. But for me, the event lingered in my mind. As I drove home after a well-needed hot yoga class, I laughed in amusement at the timing of it all.

After another two visits from the police, Zeydan agreed to start seeing a mental health nurse.

Practice Ground

During challenging times with Zeydan, there were many parenting moments of which I am not proud. When I felt attacked and unsafe to levels that exceeded my limits, instead of remaining calm and collected, I blew up and screamed at my sweet son. And each time I'd blow up, Zeydan would retreat more into himself. No amount of apologizing would undo the emotional distress I had placed on him with my immature outbursts.

Yet, it's these moments that provided me with the opportunity to return, practice, and begin again. And each time I faltered and lost it, I apologized to Zeydan for yelling, and I assured myself that next time I would remain calm and centered. So each day, I started fresh, ready to begin my practice of mastering my feelings, words, and actions.

I was diligent in my inner training and practice to be aware of my instinctive fight or flight response which would instantly activate when Zeydan started uttering accusations or name-calling. In those moments, I would quicken in my body, breathe loving assurance into my being, and consciously choose to respond to the situation with responsible assertiveness rather than emotionally immature reactivity.

Opportunity after opportunity presented itself for me to apply and refine the tools and practices that I was learning from my spiritual life coach training, my spiritual mentor, and my personal life coach. With the myriad of pressures and responsibilities I had on the go, I can't imagine how I would have coped and remained healthy and stable without the support structure I had in place. It's through these supports and a lifestyle that included yoga, the outdoors, and nourishing foods, coupled with constant mindful inward effort, that I could maintain a home that was safe for everyone. I learned to keep my inner sea calm, despite the turbulence on the surface around me.

Meanwhile, I maintained my role as a part-time lawyer, while the court saga over Asia's support and access with Seth continued. Asia was appointed a children's lawyer to represent her views in court, and this was the beginning of the end to this story. Asia was scared and unsure of the process, but she bravely met with the lawyer as needed and relayed her experiences and preferences for spending time with Seth and me.

Attempts at reconciling Seth's and Asia's relationship were made through counselling sessions that were mandated through a temporary court order. Asia was super anxious before the sessions and did not want to go, but I insisted (especially considering it was ordered by the court). She stuck to it and showed up.

For several years, she had never spoken her truth to Seth because she was afraid that he would get angry and be mad at her. But through the counselling sessions, and for the first time, Asia told her truth to Seth directly to his face: she wanted to live with me.

Note to Self: Hmm. The fear of speaking our truth and facing aggression sounds familiar, doesn't it? The apple doesn't fall far from the tree. Children model what we do, not what we say. But fear not, it's all perfect and for a purpose. Our souls chose our circumstances—parents, problems, and all.

Attempts at reconciliation through counselling were botched. After their sessions, Asia was frustrated because Seth continually brought my name into the discussions. Rather than convey sincere interest into Asia's life, Seth would regress into how I did him wrong and how all of this was my fault. Asia felt that Seth cared more about being angry at me than wanting to start fresh and mend his relationship with her.

In the end, a new final court order was issued: Asia was to reside with me full-time and was granted autonomy in choosing when she wanted to see Seth. No access schedule was stipulated. Seth could no longer attempt to force or threaten Asia to stay at his place.

Asia found her voice. She gained strength, courage, and self-confidence through the process of expressing her wishes, even if it meant hurting Seth's feelings.

Although they stopped seeing each other, Seth texted Asia occasionally, and he continued to blame me for his woes, like selling his home and getting rid of the pets so that he could afford to pay child support. Or his texts were worded in a way that stirred feelings of guilt in Asia for her choosing to live with her mother.

But Asia was mature well beyond her age, and she saw through Seth's attempts at alienation and his guilt-laden comments. These messages simply created more distance between them and they strengthened Asia's lack of desire to see Seth, let alone be at his place. Asia would only tell me of these texts long after she had received them. And despite her saying she was "fine", I suspected otherwise. She agreed to speak to a counsellor to express her thoughts and feelings, about not only losing her relationship with her dad, but also with her brother whom she adored.

Since Asia arrived on my doorstep in tears that Sunday morning many years earlier, she has never stepped into Seth's place. She hasn't received a holiday card or any type of gift from Seth since then.

Through these tumultuous times, I developed patience beyond that which I ever thought possible. I cultivated steadfast confidence in myself and my intuition and a profound sense of compassion and what truly matters in life. I uncovered parts of myself that were previously hidden and entirely foreign to me. I was mining the essence of who I really was, and the light was beginning to shine through.

CHAPTER 4

Excavating the Gem: Rising with Resilience

Only in hindsight will the miracles become obvious, will you see you were guided, and will you find there was order all along.
—*Mike Dooley, A Note from the Universe*

As the end of my eighteen-month spiritual life coach training and personal life coaching sessions came near, I became fully immersed in my studies and my inner personal work. Aside from working and managing my motherly responsibilities, I had no social life. My dating with Roger dwindled as I fell deeper in love with this passion for learning about the nature of myself and my desire to help others transcend their circumstances. I remained an avid student of George, receiving and applying instruction on spiritual and energetic principles and practices.

But what good is knowledge without application?

I still had the perfect environment in which I could apply and practice the skills and knowledge I was gaining through my studies. During heated moments of Zeydan's outbursts, I walked away and investigated my emotional reactivity and mastered my emotional responses. I built a solid foundation of faith in the harmony of life. I unattached from my desired outcomes and trusted that the highest good was always happening for all involved. I responded to life's challenging moments with compassionate concern while I maintained emotional neutrality and personal integrity.

Regardless of my external conditions, I persistently did my inner work. While completing an assignment on the roles I had played as a child, I reflected and journaled on my tendency to hide as a little girl which earned my suitable nickname of "Mousie".

It hit me like a ton of bricks—I had been playing Mousie my entire life. Memories of me as a little girl in the apartment flooded in. I saw myself run and hide under the bed, in the bathroom, and behind the curtains. I could see that I always kept my mouth shut, stifled my voice, and watched as aggression and violence went on around me.

During those moments of investigation and introspection, I realized and accepted for the first time in my life that I was petrified as a little girl and that I had every right to feel that way. But I had stifled my feelings of fright, and instead fabricated beliefs about myself and the world around me.

The repressed feelings and false beliefs remained with me through my life. They created a persona and a way of being, and as an adult, I continued to run in the face of adversity, just like I had as a little girl. I was always quiet and reserved, and I rarely spoke the truth of how I felt.

I saw how my painful relationships provided me with opportunities to step up and speak out, but instead, I chose to retreat and hide. I recalled all the animosity that I had avoided and darted around like a frightened mouse.

I saw that my life was always blessed with the steadfast support and unconditional love from my mom and sister who were there for me, no matter what, but instead, I chose to retreat inside myself and pretend I was okay and happy. I realized that I never learned how to manage my feelings and that the things that caused me discomfort and pain, were the things I didn't talk about with anyone, regardless of how loving and supportive those people were. And so I pretended that the feelings weren't there.

My beliefs about who I was had shaped my relationships, my experiences, and my entire life. And regardless of what I wanted to create in my life, I could only experience a level of fulfillment that matched my persona and the mask that I was wearing. But now, I had the skills and tools to plainly see these beliefs, investigate them, and change them—for good. And with that realization, a dam of energy surged through my body as I purged years' worth of suppressed beliefs and feelings.

At the age of forty-five, I released the old, familiar, and dysfunctional mask that I had worn. I reclaimed an identity that I lost sight of so long ago. I stopped signing my name as *Mousie* in correspondence with my family. I had a real name—it was *Christine*.

From that point forward, I committed to living with my eyes wide open—aware as to when I was acting from a story that my protective mind had conjured up that was rooted in past limiting beliefs and feelings of fear, insufficiency, and powerlessness. My faith was unwavering in that what I was experiencing was merely a result of past limiting beliefs about myself that had shaped my habits, personality, and life. I began to deliberately choose and reprogram empowering thoughts and beliefs into my mind. I became a vigilant visionary and built a new future one thought, one word, and one action at a time.

Note to Self: Whoooo hooooo!

As my studies and inner personal work deepened, I began to see how I had idealized Apu, and that I had needed to do so as a child to feel safe, like an abused dog attaches to its abuser's side. Despite his angry and hurtful outbursts, Apu could do no wrong in my young and scared eyes. I also saw how I had enmeshed with and modeled after my mom, from her hard working, loving, and dedicated traits to her old beliefs of powerlessness.

I began to see others' behaviours as just that, their *behaviours*—a result of their limited thinking and beliefs based on how they were raised and the traumas and emotional shocks they had experienced in their lives. I saw beneath people's personas and masks, where only God's love resides.

I gained a profound understanding and deep appreciation and respect that everyone has a story that is true for them; that every life presents precisely what is needed for people to see their beliefs and mind-made stories; and that everyone's experiences are there to transcend and learn from, as I had done (eventually) with mine. And that people and their stories interweave with one another to awaken to greater parts of themselves, and that without each other, personal growth would be nearly impossible.

I also respected that each person has a choice on their journey: they can learn from their experiences and transcend them, or not—the choice is theirs, and theirs alone to make.

I started seeing everyone as me, a Child of God, a soul coming to experience life and to grow more fully into their greatness. The homeless person on the street. The driver who cut me off on the road. The shopper who butted in front of me in line. The criminal who had assaulted the innocent.

I saw that we are all the same, and despite our mind's tendency to judge, we are all trying the best we can given our past experiences and current circumstances—in fact, we are all acting righteously according to our own beliefs.

And with these deep realizations, I silently appreciated and honoured the men in my life who reflected that which I was holding on to. They helped to awaken my strength and power, and without each of them, I would not be the strong and driven woman that I am today.

I found a deep love for everyone—yes, a hippie in the making. I started saying "I love you", and meant it, to people I barely knew. I started hugging strangers with whom I'd strike up a meaningful conversation in passing. I discovered deep reverence for all of life, even the seemingly bad things, because underneath it all I saw perfection.

For the first time in my life, I had learned about boundaries and how to maturely defend them—although, as I grew into my self-mastery, I rarely felt the need to do so.

A New Groove

One afternoon, Zeydan left for a counselling appointment with his mental health nurse. Shortly after he left for his appointment, I received multiple texts from him repeatedly asking me to "Please just tell the truth."

Moments later, the phone rang. It was Family and Children's Services calling. My heart sank. *Oh no. Here we go again.*

But instead of feeling dismay over this unexpected and certainly unwanted call, by the end of it I felt pride and amazement over what Zeydan had just done.

After the nurse and psychiatrist threatened to report Zeydan to Family and Children's Services for not wanting to take medication, he marched out of their office and walked straight to the police station to report the mental health office for extortion. He then proactively called Family and Children's Services to convince them that he was not a threat in the home.

After a few minutes of answering questions with the woman from Family and Children's Services, she assured me that she had no reason to be involved.

When Zeydan returned home later that day, I commended him for taking action and standing up for himself. I assured him that Family and Children's Services were gone for good.

Zeydan lost trust in his nurse that day and ended his counselling sessions with her.

With a newfound level of patience and appreciation for Zeydan's journey, we got into a new groove at home. I took the times Zeydan acted out as an opportunity to master my conscious choice of thoughts, feelings, words, and actions and respond with mature emotional stability rather than child-like defenses. It took considerable effort and lots of practice.

And there were times when I slipped back into old defensive ways. But, I was kind to myself and simply vowed to remain more conscious with the next opportunity.

Although we were in this new groove, the environment at home was not an open and airy one. The heaviness from Zeydan's suspicions and occasional accusations lingered in the atmosphere. The tension could be felt. Although I managed to refine and develop my ability to respond to escalated outbursts, I proceeded with caution in the home—to avoid triggering Zeydan.

In our new relationship at home, Zeydan was like a tenant whom I rarely saw. The old regimented me would have insisted on him picking up after himself and doing his own laundry. I would have tried to control him to "do as I say" while "living under my roof." But with a newfound level of compassion and understanding, and insight into my old thoughts which no longer served me or Zeydan, I lightened up and loosened up and continued to provide for his living essentials with gratitude for his health and presence in the home.

Zeydan enjoyed cooking, and he was great at it, so when he'd offer to cook a meal, I jumped for joy on the inside. I loved seeing the pride with which he created seasonings and marinades for the vegetables and meats and the care and focus he applied when he'd tend to them on the barbeque. I could see the passion and a small spark of joy light in him when he cooked, and I reveled in watching him do so.

A few months before Zeydan's eighteenth birthday, we began the process for Zeydan to apply for provincial financial support, which his mental health nurse had suggested in the past. Although he was no longer in her care, she graciously completed the in-depth application for Zeydan.

Within months of the application being submitted, a letter addressed by the government program arrived in the mail. I eagerly passed it to Zeydan, and he beamed with excitement as he opened the letter and saw the stamp of approval. He expressed his surprise and deep thanks that the government had awarded him this support. I was happy to see Zeydan so excited and grateful.

Later that afternoon, he somberly asked me, "Can't I just stay here and pay you rent?"

A firm, yet gentle, "No," was my reply.

"Why not?"

"Zeydan," I continued kindly, "it's not really comfortable for any of us at home, I think it would be best for all of us if you moved out. You've always wanted to do things on your own and live by your own rules. This is your opportunity."

"Can I keep the keys to the house?"

"No. But you are always welcome, and you always have a home here. With Asia here, I need notice. You can't just walk in."

Hands-down, those were the most difficult words I had uttered in my life.

Later that night in the privacy of my room, I reflected on the decisions I had made and wept with torment. Asia and I weren't comfortable walking on eggshells. For so long, I had sought a home that was happy, rejuvenating, and comforting—and with the accusations and random outbursts from Zeydan, the air was tense and apprehensive. But as a mother to my son, I was devasted to tell him these things and ask him to leave home—again. My firstborn. My sweet, sweet Zeydan.

Within a few weeks of receiving news of the financial support, we searched online for apartments for rent. We bonded and connected as we browsed ads together and discussed the possibilities that unfolded before him. I was happy to see Zeydan eager and optimistic in his search. We found an affordable one-bedroom apartment about fifteen minutes from our house and quickly set an appointment to view it.

We entered the humble two-story, twelve-unit building and made our way to the superintendent's door. I was relieved to see the building was kempt. An older, kindly gentleman answered our knocks. As we walked with the superintendent through the hallway, I made small talk with him of his life as a superintendent, sharing my related experiences from childhood.

We stepped into the vacant unit. I stopped and glanced around the spacious, clean, and bright space with conflicting feelings. I was relieved that the unit was clean, and the building was well maintained by this caring man, yet at the same time, I worried about my son living on his own.

After admiring the apartment, we followed the superintendent back to his apartment, Zeydan spoke under his breath, "I like it. This is the one. Can we get it?"

Bearing in mind Zeydan's recent tendency to change his mind on a whim, I reminded him, "You need to be one hundred percent sure of this. Once we sign the lease, we can't change our minds. There is no backing out once I give cheques for first and last month's rent."

Entirely eager, Zeydan assured me, "I'm positive. This is the one. It feels good. I want to get it."

A battle ensued between my mind and heart. I didn't know whether to be delighted or dismayed. But I felt assured that Zeydan would be in good hands with this kind man on the lookout for Zeydan's wellbeing.

"Okay, we'll take it!"

Zeydan was motivated and excited. He had always yearned to have his own place and to do as he pleased without having to abide by anyone's rules. Even as a child, he disliked receiving instruction from his guitar and swimming instructors and veered from their directions. So, during the weeks approaching his move, Zeydan worked eagerly and diligently searching buy-and-sell ads to get the pieces needed to furnish his new home.

The day before the planned move, Zeydan beamed with excitement when we finally got clearance to collect the apartment key from the superintendent. With a freshly steam-cleaned living room carpet and polished floors, the apartment was ready for us to begin moving things in. Zeydan was tremendously eager to settle into his new place, so after we made a few trips bringing essential supplies, like food, the television, and the Xbox, Zeydan slept the first night in his new home in a sleeping bag and pillow on his living room floor.

The following morning, Roger helped as we jammed the large moving van that I had rented. Asia made her fair share of trips to and from the moving van and up and down the stairs of Zeydan's building until the last of Zeydan's items were moved into his apartment. Once the van was emptied, we ate some subs in Zeydan's new place before bidding him farewell.

Three months after his eighteenth birthday, Zeydan moved into his apartment.

Thoughts of Zeydan as a toddler grinning from ear to ear, giggling with glee, and running into my arms filled my mind. We spent countless times together and shared treasured experiences as mother and son. We were inseparable. Never would I have imagined that my relationship with him would turn out as it had that day. Never would I have imagined insisting that my sweet son leave home at the naïve age of eighteen. I mourned the dissolution of my past relationship with my son, unsure of what the future held for him and our relationship.

Note to Self: Oh, Love. As a mother, this understandably was an agonizing decision and situation to endure because our children are so dear and special to us. You are doing the best you can. All is well.

Rising

When Zeydan initially moved into his apartment, I visited and helped with minor things, like setting up a bookshelf and installing curtain rods. But after the initial set up was complete, Zeydan stopped answering my texts and my knocks on his door. Still, I continued to drop off food and supplies at his door regularly. Long gone was my past belief that I needed to hear a "thank you" from someone when I gave them something. I dropped my need to feel appreciated, and in its place was deep compassion for what my sweet son must have been experiencing, mentally and emotionally. All that remained in me was deep unconditional love to support him through his process.

After a few months passed, I began to immensely appreciate any sign of life from Zeydan, like the texts I'd receive from him requesting the financial support that I gave him monthly. With each text message, I'd breathe a sigh of relief knowing that my son was alive and, at the least, paying his bills.

With time and space, Zeydan began answering his door again, and ever since, we've established a routine, whereby the same day each week, I drop off food at his place—groceries, take-out, or homemade food, or some combination therein. We chat for mere moments in the doorway of his apartment, skimming the surface of matters. When I ask how he's doing, Zeydan's response is, "Great."

When I peer into his apartment from his doorway, I see that he's rearranged his furniture again. I smile to myself as I spot a new mirror on the wall. At times, he proudly points out new things he's purchased like new cushions for his couch, a new picture for his wall, or a new bathrobe.

On Valentine's Day last year, he opened his door and engaged in more conversation than usual, asking me several times what I was doing. Picking up on his subtle gestures, I offered to take him for dinner. Before I could finish my invitation, he zealously accepted. And for almost two hours at a local Thai restaurant, we ate and talked. I did my best to keep up with the conversation and the things of which Zeydan spoke. I was simply delighted to be sharing the time and space with him and offer a kind ear and word. During our conversation, I'd circle back to things at home, and tell him the latest events that Asia, Cheeko, and I had been up to.

Almost a year has passed since our extended conversation over dinner that evening, and I continue to see Zeydan weekly in his doorway.

When friends and family ask me, "How is Zeydan?"

My response is, "If I were to say how, I would be making a judgment that may or may not be accurate. What I can tell you for certain is what I hear and see. He looks well, and he says he's great."

The next question is usually, "So what does he do all day? Is he going to school?"

To which my response is, "I'm not sure. He probably hangs out with friends and plays video games. The grocery store is two kilometers away, so he bikes, walks, or takes the bus there. And he likely plays a lot of music as well... he's amazing at playing the guitar."

My level of acceptance and my open, factual response regarding my son's lifestyle and my relationship with him, leaves most people feeling uncomfortable. The conversation usually ends abruptly with people quickly changing the topic or suddenly finding something they have to get to.

Through my inner work and experiences, I have come to wholeheartedly believe that each of us has our own journey in this collective project called LIFE in which we've all embarked. And as a parent, my children came through me, but not for me. As much as I want my children to "succeed" in life, as young adults they have a right to make their own choices and experience the natural effects of those choices. And when my attempts to sway (or perhaps force) their decisions are consistently met with resistance and create more havoc than harmony, then I take a step back and ask myself, "What exactly am I enforcing and why? How critical is this in the big picture of life?"

Creating Happiness

Zeydan is living a humble life supported financially by the government with some help from family. He gets to live life *his way*, something he always yearned to have and experience when he was younger. He's carved out his definition of happy, and he's likely happier than a large percentage of people in modernized society.

Do I believe he's living his greatest life now? No. But, he has a whole lifetime ahead of him with loving and caring family who are eager to help him when he is ready. His wit, determination, creativity, and talents will carry him through and shine forth in perfect timing.

To me, Zeydan is as successful as any young adult who has graduated from university with honours because Zeydan is doing *him*. He's not trying to be somebody he's not just to please others and to comply with the generally accepted norm.

His journey has provided him with massive lessons to gain and amazing qualities to realize, and when he grasps these immense lessons, he will transform the lives of many if he chooses to share his message with the world.

As I learned from Dr. Sue Morter, big souls choose big projects.

We all want to be happy, right?

Happiness looks different to different people. Fundamentally to all though, happiness merely means that one has feelings of wellbeing and contentment.

Throughout most of my adult life, happy is not what I was. I believed that happiness was something that I needed to find, and I desperately searched for it. And occasionally, I'd find it momentarily through my relationships with my partners, friends, family, and children. But when my loved one acted out or was upset or angry, my happiness disappeared. There was no separation between my emotions and the emotions of those who were close to me—I was enmeshed. And when my happiness was sourced from material things, like a new house, it quickly faded into feelings of dissatisfaction, impatience, and overwhelm. My happiness was fleeting, variable, and dependent on other people and things outside of myself and my control.

Through my journey in this Project: LIFE, I've found the source of my happiness—it was in me all along, completely independent of any external factor, including friends, jobs, money, weather, family, and my own children.

Through mining my internal terrain, I became able to discern subtle energetic drains in my surroundings and refrain from engaging with them. I realized that my relationship with Roger needed to end. I had grown and expanded so much that I became a different me. I became a me that desired the unseen—deeply intimate, emotional, and spiritual connection. I realized that my passion was in sharing the empowering tools that I had so graciously learned and utilized through life, and I began focusing much of my time toward growing my coaching business.

Roger remains a dear and trusted friend in my life, whom I adore immensely.

Nico attempted to be my "friend" on Facebook. And though I had released energetic ties with him, I consciously declined the invite. Some associations are better left as severed—this is also the case in my relationship with Seth.

I remain in touch with Paul, his wife, and his parents, as we all continue to process our LIFE projects and the impact that Zeydan's journey has had on our desires and our minds' attachments to how each of our relationships with Zeydan *should* be. We all share hope and a profound prayer that Zeydan's inner strength and determination will shine through soon, so he can once again become an active part of our lives. We all miss him dearly.

Asia remains living with me and Cheeko full-time. She's maturing into a wise young woman, and she continues to be one of my greatest teachers.

Today, Marcus and Mom are like two teens in love. Marcus remains the knight that sparks the twinkle in Mom's eyes. Angelina and her supportive husband remain together living with their young adult children. And Mom and Angelina continue to provide the unconditional love and support that had been constant throughout my life.

Every person in my life has played a role in my journey and my becoming the me I am today. Each experience, painful or otherwise, was a necessary piece that completed the intricate puzzle in my Project: LIFE.

Through the most trying and painful circumstances, I've mined priceless gems within the depths of my soul—gems that would have remained buried had life not have painfully blasted access to them. And it was through these seemingly bad situations that I could clear the debris and embrace the glimmer of light which was attempting to burst through to reveal life's genuine treasure.

And for the trying and painful circumstances and the people who played their necessary parts in my project, I am profoundly grateful.

Despite not drinking a drop of alcohol or consuming any drugs, I live an intoxicated life. I'm high on energy and happiness eighteen hours a day.

I've finally unearthed an endless and constant source of unconditional happiness and love. It's not tied to a physical person or a place. It involves no body and no thing outside of me. It's a state of being—one that I access anytime and anywhere and with anyone. It's happy.

It's home.

PART 2

YOUR STORY: *LIFE*

CHAPTER 5

Listen: What is Your Life Telling You?

Opportunity is missed by most people because it is dressed in overalls and looks like work.

—*Thomas Edison*

Don't be sad.

I'll give you something to cry about.

Crying is for babies.

Don't do that, or Dad will get angry.

Any of those sound familiar?

If, like me, you were taught to believe that certain feelings were wrong, then chances are you (unknowingly) repress, deny, or minimize your feelings, and have been for most of your life.

Rest assured, this is by no fault of your own.

I associated anger as bad. I mean, I watched Apu, my stepdad, get angry, and the result was someone or something paid the price—bleeding lips, black eyes, broken glass. You get the idea. So anytime I sensed Apu's anger bubbling up, I ran and hid like a mouse, and simultaneously and subconsciously my mind filed anger into a bucket of bad things to avoid at all costs. I ignored and denied my feelings of anger throughout my life, and I avoided aggressive people and confrontational situations—yet these are precisely what appeared in my life. Repeatedly.

Despite being punched by my boyfriend, Nico, and being emotionally, verbally, mentally, and sexually abused by my partner, Seth, I never once felt angry.

I walked around with a forced smile on my face, and my children would call me on it at times, "Mom, you're angry."

My response? "No, I'm not."

OMG. Of course I was angry! My protective mind was convincing me otherwise because of my negative association with anger. I was in denial, and I didn't even know it.

Feelings aren't good, bad, right, or wrong. They're just feelings. Yet, our parents and society have taught us that it's terrible to feel heavy emotions, like anger or sadness. At some point in our lives, we've all had people try to make us feel happy and to get us to laugh in an attempt to stop us from crying and feeling sad—just like I attempted to do with my mom at my dad's funeral. Feeling sad doesn't feel good, it's no wonder we want to avoid it!

Did your caretakers or early life influencers openly express their feelings? Was crying and expressing your feelings of displeasure welcomed and encouraged?

If you're a student of mine and you're feeling sad, I say, "Great! Feel it!"

Here's why…

Open to Possibilities

Before the why, I'll provide a little primer to help with your journey in this part of the book. Personal growth comes when we learn new things, and learning new things requires an openness to new ideas. It requires us to, at least momentarily, entertain possibilities that we may not believe—yet.

If you're familiar with my work or recent work on the science of spirituality, then what I'm about to share will not be news to you. But if you're somewhat skeptical, then you may well think I'm insane. And that's okay. I realize that what I present here may be a far stretch for some based on that which mainstream society has taught through our schools, systems, and institutions. If you fall into this category, then perhaps play along for a moment and pretend. You'll lose nothing and stand to gain a new perspective and insight.

No biggie.

As you journey through this section of the book, pay attention to and tame the doubts and judgments that automatically arise within you when you encounter something that is unfamiliar or contradicts your beliefs.

Perhaps you had similar judgments and emotions arise if you read the first part—My Story.

Before discrediting something, consider possibility.

Be open.

Are you ready?

We Are Energy

Modern science has proven beyond doubt that all matter is energy—including us humans. That's right. Under a microscope, we are simply a collection of protons, neutrons, and electrons vibrating in space.

Did you catch that?

We're mostly just space.

I know, right?!

Our bodies are comprised of compressed neutrons, protons, and electrons (energy) that are animated to life through Spirit and God's Will. Each one of us—as our True Essence/ Higher Self—is an Individualization of God Consciousness (a drop in God's vast ocean) and we're here having a spiritual experience on Earth. We are Spiritual Energy Beings playing the role of a human.

I use the word Higher Self to refer to our True Essence, and by higher I'm not necessarily referring to physicality, but rather a level of consciousness/awareness or vibration of our energy. The Higher Self is also commonly referred to as True Self, Inner Self, I AM Presence, Soulful Self, and Soul (which technically is a little different, but that doesn't concern us at this point). Similarly, I refer to "God", which for some means Universe, Creator, Allah, etc.—basically, the creative and governing force of existence, regardless of the name we ascribe to it.

More and more people are accepting, realizing, and, yes, experiencing that in a state of elevated consciousness, we are one with God. Through our unity with our Higher Selves, we have the same divine qualities as God, just as our DNA has the same traits as our parents' DNA.

We Have a Protective Self

As Spiritual Energy Beings, we incarnated into human form to undertake this grand project of LIFE to experience and master aspects of ourselves and fully realize our divine qualities, mainly creatorship. We knew this when we were born, but we learned otherwise from our caregivers and society, and eventually, we entirely forgot about the nature and purpose of our voyage and existence.

We forgot about our divine nature and inheritance and began to think that we were other things, like our bodies, thoughts, feelings, and the roles we played. We believed that we were an effect of the causes outside of us, rather than being the creators of our worlds and experiences. Each one of us developed a mental construct of who we thought we were. We developed a protective personality and a false sense of self, which I'll refer to as the ego (or ego mind), and we believed that we were our egos. And unless we were taught otherwise by awakened caregivers or mentors, our egos led our lives rather than our Higher Selves.

As adults, our egos are like overly-sensitive bodyguards protecting us from potential threats—physical, mental, or emotional—whether real or imagined. Despite what you may think, our egos aren't the bad guys, they're merely doing their jobs helping us feel safe, sane, secure, and in control, especially when things are anything but. But that which our egos perceive as potentially harmful is just that: a perception based purely on experiences and beliefs from the past. These beliefs have stuck with us in the present, even though the present is decades later with completely different circumstances to which past experiences and beliefs no longer apply. More on that later.

We are *not* our thoughts, feelings, or bodies, or the roles we play in life—these are things we *have*. Just like we have a car, a house, and a job. We are Spiritual Energy Beings that have a physical body and an ego, so we can function in this world.

So, back to why I think it's great to feel sad.

Feelings—the Language of Our Soul

Feelings are a normal part of our human experience, and they're necessary to help us navigate life. If you're like me, you've believed that feelings are the same as emotions, but these, in fact, are different.

Wait. What?

Emotions, such as angry, sad, and happy, are generalized cognitive labels that we ascribe to a feeling we're experiencing. Feelings have an energy vibration associated with them, which when paid close attention to can be felt as a tactile/physical sensation in the body, such as heavy, light, soft, hard, tight, loose, or tingling. Feelings and emotions are experienced in different parts of the brain.

Feelings physically *feel* a certain way in our bodies. When we feel energy in our bodies that is vibrating at a slower rate, it might feel heavy and tight, and we may interpret, label, and describe it as sad or angry. When we feel energy in our bodies that is vibrating at a faster rate, it might feel light and airy, and we may label it as happy.

Makes sense, yes?

There's yet another aspect to feelings. We also have gut feelings that are experienced in a third area of the brain. Our gut feelings comprise our hunches, intuition, or sixth sense and are usually the subtlest to detect.

> **Our bodies and feelings never lie, so we can always depend on them to tell us the truth.**

Feelings are like our internal thermostats for our personal development and growth. They act as our guideposts: how our Higher Selves communicate with us to let us know when we're veering off the path. The beauty of this communication system is that our bodies and feelings never lie, so we can always depend on them to tell us the truth, and they will always guide us in a way that serves our highest purpose and leads us on our ideal path.

I want to mention here that there are limitless paths and that no path is right or wrong. All roads lead to the same place, but one road may be bumpy, exhausting, ice cold, and time-consuming, while another may be paved, downhill, warm, and breezy lined with lemonade stands along the way. All paths simply provide us with experiences as we head toward our destination of self-realization and mastery of our worlds.

The apparent flaw in this communication system is that our minds step in, take over, and lie to us about our feelings. The mind (mis)interprets, judges, and defends our actions and those of others while simultaneously repressing, denying, and minimizing our feelings about them—as I did with the feeling of anger for most of my life. This is simply a function of our egos: to protect us and keep us feeling safe and comfortable including keeping us from feeling our heavier emotions, which don't feel good in the body.

Also consider that our minds often try to think our feelings rather than feel them in our bodies. It's another defense system that the ego uses to keep us from feeling painful feelings. Think (ironically) about that for a moment. If you're asked how you feel, you likely think, *Hmm, how am I feeling?* Or, you don't think at all and simply blurt out, "fine," "good," or "okay."

How often do you take a moment to pause and feel physical sensations in your body and truly connect to how you are *actually* feeling?

Feelings Originate from Within

To help illustrate the next point, stop for a moment, and do the following activity.

Like, actually do this:

1. Take three long, slow, deep breaths.

2. Think of someone or something, such as a partner or a pet, that you love dearly.

3. See them in your mind's eye and picture them in their best behaviour. Visualize the fine details of their appearance and their wonderful character traits. Allow the feeling of love to expand and surround you. Become immersed in it.

4. Simply feel.

How does your body feel?

We're looking for physical sensations here: perhaps warm, tingling, or open and expansive.

Got it?

And now...

1. Think of a person or a time where you were upset or angry.

2. Recap the event and all the details of it. Who said what, where, when, and how?

3. Simply feel.

What physical sensations does your body feel?

Is there a place in your back or throat that feels tight or knotted? Maybe there's pounding in your heart. Maybe there's fluttering in your stomach. There's no right or wrong answer here. The idea is to observe and listen to your internal sensing and feeling capacities. Whatever the feeling, know that it is simply energy in the body vibrating at a certain rate.

Now, go back to that vision of the beloved person or pet. See them in your mind's eye and picture their features and all the minor details of them. The way they smile (yes, some pets smile). The way they smell. The way they look. Feel the love. Feel appreciation and gratitude for them. Let those feelings soak into your cells and overcome you.

Who created those feelings? Was it the person or pet you visualized?

Nope.

You created them!

The vision you generated in your mind helped to surface those feelings, and since you produced the image at will, by pure logic, you generated those feelings. No one gave them to you. No one, but you, created them. And you have the ability and power to call forth those feelings of love at any moment.

So, just to be clear, no one *makes* you feel angry. It already exists within you as dense energy. People or events merely bring it forth for you to be aware of and resolve...

... or repress and deny.

When is the last time you said to someone, "You're making me feel _____"?

You are the source of your feelings, the so-called good and the bad. Without question. This is terrible news for your ego because you can no longer blame people for your feelings!

Sorry. The cat's out of the bag.

But there's excellent news! This also means that you have the ability and power to change your feelings, exactly as you did a moment ago (unless you cheated and didn't do the activity) through pausing, visualizing, and physically sensing.

> **When the vibration of love or gratitude is present in your body, it's impossible to feel heavy feelings.**

When the vibration of love or gratitude is present in your body, it's impossible to feel heavy feelings. There's great power in this!

Did you catch that?

When your feelings are heavy and running amok, go through that little exercise and generate a feeling of love in your body. Create a vision—your happy place—that you can access at will. It's a learned skill. With practice, it comes quite easily.

Love truly conquers all.

Be Sad

We just learned that each feeling (the so-called good and the bad), has an energetic frequency or vibration associated with it that is experienced as a physical or tactile sensation in the body. But, because we've been taught that heavier feelings and emotions, like sadness, are wrong, we've learned to block them. We don't allow them to surface and be in motion—instead we repress or deny them and pretend we're not feeling them.

I'm fine. Ahem.

Sound familiar?

I'm sure I'm not the only one who has said that!

Our feelings are simply energy. Emotions are just energy in motion. Keyword is *motion*. Feeling our feelings and releasing them keeps our energy flowing. Like water trapped in a stream, energy that is blocked in our bodies becomes stagnant and stale. The consequence is dis-ease within our bodies and lives.

So, finally (for real), here's why I think it's great when people are sad.

It means they're allowing their feelings to be felt and to flow! It means they're being emotionally honest with themselves, and they aren't letting their minds come up with lies to convince them otherwise and to block their feelings. When the energy of those feelings is moving and flowing, they're heading toward the paved path.

Feelings are meant to be acknowledged and moved through us, just as food assimilates and passes through us. I mean, it's beautiful and healthy to be emotionally honest and feel sad, but who wants to feel sad? It doesn't feel good. It kind of sucks.

So, feel it and let it flow!

But the key is to *release* it, and let it pass through you rather than remain in you. Cry. Laugh. Breathe. Bring your conscious attention to the space that is holding the energy of the feeling and breathe loving presence into that area of the body. We'll cover this in more detail later.

All feelings, the so-called good and the bad, are a normal and natural part of our human experience, and each feeling benefits us when we acknowledge it and allow it to flow through us. For instance:

- Feeling sad may help us create closure so that we can move on healthily. When we repress or block our feelings of sadness, depression usually results.

- Feeling scared may help us start something new, while blocking our scared feelings leads us to procrastinate.

- Feeling angry may help us assert our boundaries (which I could have used more of throughout my life). And when we block our anger, blaming others is a common vice.

Yes, denser emotions, like anger and sadness, don't feel good at the time, and the ego will try to spare us from the pain of experiencing them by externalizing, blaming, and taking it out on others. But it's better to experience and release feelings, as uncomfortable as they may feel, for ten minutes than to block and repress them and endure the consequences of the blocked energy for years (or even decades) to come. Repressing and denying feelings cause the energy of them to become stuck and blocked within us, and life will provide us with repeated opportunities to coerce those feelings to surface, for as many times as needed for the energy to flow freely once again. Repressing and denying feelings costs us our physical/mental health and happiness.

When you sense, feel, and listen to the softer nudges and subtler clues in your body and life, it won't take pain (PAIN: Pay Attention Inward Now), an appendix rupture, or a catastrophic life event to get your full inward attention.

But, listening, allowing, and following our feelings doesn't mean we're going to experience instant bliss. Eventually, perhaps. But let's take it one step at a time.

After I finally listened to and followed my feelings and split from each of my abusive partners, I experienced intense heavy emotions. These feelings and emotions were simply a part of my healing process that allowed me to get closure on the relationships. The feelings passed, and I felt great after.

You have an option and a choice.

Pay attention before the pain!

Listen, acknowledge, and allow your feelings to flow!

Be sad!

To be able to do this effectively, we need to practice and develop our ability to observe and listen. You'd think this is easy, but this isn't necessarily the case. Most of us have lost this ability and we need to practice and rehabilitate our senses, so we can begin to hear and follow our bodies' clues.

What do we practice?

Meditation—Develop Your Inner Listening Skills

We were raised in a doing society, where success is based on bigger, better, faster, stronger, and smarter, and to get there, we need to work harder, accumulate more things, achieve more, and do it all faster. If we're not doing something, we risk being frowned upon or labelled by society or our loved ones as being lazy or not trying hard enough. Through the process of speeding through life to succeed and accumulate things and information, our minds took over and ran the show while our senses atrophied.

If you don't use it, you lose it.

Just as we engage in regular strength training to build muscles, so too do we engage in daily meditation training to develop our inner listening skills. When we do so, we quiet and train the noisy mind to steer away from the bigger, better, faster, stronger.

In the past, one was labelled as a hippie for mentioning meditation. Today, mindfulness and meditation are common terms that celebrities are beginning to promote and speak openly of.

So, what is meditation?

It's simply being with ourselves in the absence of external stimuli and placing our focus and attention inwardly using our breath. Numerous scientific studies have proven several physiological benefits of meditation, but the greatest benefit comes in the development of our self-awareness and self-mastery over our thoughts, words, feelings, and actions. And it's these primary benefits that trickle into all areas of our lives and manifest as greater health, loving relationships, abundant energy, and more happiness and ease.

Through meditation, our minds learn to focus on the inside rather than the outside. And as we do this, we begin to sense communications from our Higher Selves (our intuition) and start to notice our gut instincts as easily as we do a sore throat. Eventually, we master the art of mindful living, and we receive these higher communications throughout our active lives, not just while we're sitting in meditation. And when we sense and follow communications from our Higher Selves, life becomes fantastic!

The purpose of meditation is to train your mind to pay attention and listen to you—the Real You. The mind has been running the show, and it's got you to where you are today. If you want your life to change for the better, it's

> **The mind makes a poor master, but a fantastic servant.**

time for your Higher Self to take the steering wheel and let the ego mind sit in the back seat and take directions from You.

The mind makes a poor master, but a fantastic servant—it merely needs to be trained as such.

Meditation can look like many things for many people. Some people focus their mind on their breathing while sitting or walking. Some people repeat phrases/mantras, while others follow guided meditations. I include some basic suggestions here that have helped settle my "monkey mind" and have increased my awareness and my ability to observe and master my thoughts, feelings, and actions rather than believe I am those things and let them run my life.

Sit and Be Still

To begin, sit on the floor in a full cross-legged lotus pose.

Just kidding.

You can scrap the classic cross-legged-sitting-on-a-cushion meditation pose. Not necessary. But, if you love a lotus-esque pose, go for it! Do what feels good in your body. Ideally, your spine is erect, and the muscles in your body are soft and relaxed. Be comfortable. This might mean sitting on the edge of a cushion, chair, or couch. Have a blanket near if you tend to get chilly.

Some people walk and meditate. That's cool. Hot yoga is my greatest meditation, which kind of goes against the whole "be still" idea—but it amplifies my ability to focus my mind on my breath to help me endure fierce poses in extreme heat.

Next, close your eyes to help maintain an inward focus. If you must keep your eyes open, focus on an object low and in front of you so your eyes and lids can be relaxed. Some people gaze at a flame or a mandala. Do what feels good and right for you.

Be Quiet—Outside and In

Next, stop talking—externally and internally. This is the trickiest part for most people because the mind is accustomed to wandering. Rein it in by giving it something on which to focus. Start with noticing all the sounds you hear, and strain to hear the faintest sound. Next, bring your focus to smell—what does the air or your sleeve smell like? Then bring your attention to your body. Notice any physical sensations that stand out, without getting into why they may feel that way. Can you feel your bottom or your feet resting on a surface? Is your body cold or hot?

Next, give the mind something subtler on which to focus: your breath. Slow your breathing down and place your attention on it. Notice how it feels coming in and going out of the body.

Focusing and slowing the mind is the toughest part of meditation for many. The initial goal of meditation is not to stop our thoughts. It's perfectly okay and normal for thoughts to arise during meditation. A freight train can't stop in an instant, and so it is with our thoughts. We think at least sixty thousand thoughts a day! They will not suddenly stop when we sit down to meditate. Expect your thoughts to continue, at least initially.

But here's the thing. Don't get sucked into the thoughts. Observe and notice them. When a thought arises like, *I think I'll make salad for dinner*, notice the thought: *Oh look, there's a thought*, and then let it pass without your attention. The thought may run away and self-perpetuate with you sucked in it: *I need to go to the store and get spinach and peppers. I should probably get gas on the way. Darnit, where's my new credit card? It's probably in that pile of papers. Argh, I can't believe Billy didn't clean up that pile yet… he's so messy.*

When (not if, but when) this happens, return your attention to your breath. And if that's difficult, take it back a level and return to noticing your physical senses, like the tactile sensations felt in the body.

Breathe

This is a big one!

Breath is the most important thing to human existence, yet it's something of which most of us have little awareness and we take it for granted because we weren't taught its importance, benefits, or powers. Breathing is an automatic function of our bodies, but, unlike other automated body functions, we can alter our breath with focused attention, and herein lies its power because breath is the link that unites the mind and body.

Not just any breath though—deep belly breath. The belly should inflate like a balloon on the inhale and deflate with the belly button pressing toward the spine on the exhale. For some, this takes practice.

If you're like, *Huh? My lungs aren't in my belly*, then place a hand on your belly while lying down and focus on getting it to expand while you inhale. The belly expanding is a natural effect of the diaphragm pressing down on the abdominal cavity to draw air deep into the lower lobes of the lungs. When we breathe in the upper lobes of the lungs, the diaphragm doesn't get involved. Deep belly breathing is a matter of exercising the diaphragmatic muscle.

Aside from increased blood and lymphatic flow, deep, rhythmic belly breathing overrides the primitive/reactive part of the brain by slowing down our brain waves and activating the parasympathetic nerves in the lower lobes of the lungs, which signals to our bodies that it's time to relax, rest, and digest. In addition to the beneficial physiological changes, our slowed breath also gives our minds something on which to focus.

Lastly, use your nose to breathe, not only during meditation but throughout your entire day and night. Nose breathing filters foreign particles from the air and it conditions the air to make it humid and temperate for our bodies to assimilate. It also naturally assists in the slowing of the breath and thus promotes deeper breathing.

The mouth was made for eating—breathe through your nose!

When I breathe with mindful awareness during my yoga class, I have achieved the goal of the class. Similarly, if you could do just one thing during meditation, this would be it.

Breathe.

Deeply.

Repeat

There is some benefit in meditating occasionally, and there is immense benefit in meditating regularly. It's better to meditate for five minutes a day five days a week, rather than for thirty minutes once a week. If you're a beginner, perhaps commit to five minutes daily.

Ideally, you work up to twenty or thirty minutes daily because after around twenty minutes, your thoughts start to automatically slow down. Yes, eventually, they do slow down, but don't strive for that to be your goal. When our thoughts slow, we deepen our inner awareness and our connection to our Higher Selves.

I get it, you're busy, and you don't have time to meditate, but please believe that carving out time to be still, be silent, and breathe will create more time in your day. I know it sounds slightly nuts, but it's true—time is malleable. I've experienced it, and, at some point, you have too. Have you ever said, "Wow, that was a long day," when in fact it was no longer than the day before? Have you noticed that when you're frantically rushing around that life speeds up with you?

With a meditation practice in place, we intuit much easier and more often, and when we act on those hunches, the pieces of our life puzzle begin to fall effortlessly into place. Our loved ones also benefit from our practice because we engage and listen with conscious attention, greater presence, and expanded patience. And not only that, but their energy begins to shift and align with our calmer state of energy by means of synchronicity—energy is contagious!

Keep at it! Every day.

Is It Working?

That's it! Pretty simple, right?

1. Sit and be still.

2. Be quiet—outside and in. Focus your mind on your breath. Witness your thoughts without getting sucked into them and return your attention to the breath when your mind runs astray.

3. Inhale and exhale through your nose. Slowly and deeply inflating and deflating your belly.

4. Repeat.

I knew meditation was beneficial and straightforward, but my mind told me I couldn't do it and that I didn't need to do it. My mind told me that I knew how to meditate because I had read about it for fifteen years. My mind convinced me that I didn't have enough time to meditate. And then, when I finally sat down to meditate, I thought it wasn't working and that it was useless. I became frustrated and believed that I had a "monkey mind" and that I could never meditate and quiet my thoughts. And so, I stopped trying.

Meditation is simple but not necessarily easy. It takes willpower, determination, and commitment to persist and do it despite the ego's resistance. My ego was clearly in control of my actions, and it stayed in control when it came to my personal growth and life.

Rest assured, encountering resistance from your ego is typical and expected. Assure your mind that it's okay to resist and doubt the process and that you're going to do it anyway and just see what happens. No expectations. If you think it's not working or that you're not doing it properly, trust that you are right on track. Such a response is the mind's natural reaction to this new way of being. If you've ever learned a new skill, like dancing or playing an instrument, you're familiar with the initial awkward feeling that arises when you first begin something new. But, as you keep at it and practice, the activity begins to feel natural. The same thing will happen with meditation. Guaranteed! Simply know that if you're following the basic steps outlined, you're doing it correctly!

Remember, it's not about stopping your thoughts. Simply be aware of the thoughts and allow them to pass, just like a cloud floating by—just don't sit on the cloud and ride it (although I'm sure that would be awesome).

Explore meditation with curiosity. Begin each session with innocence—as if each time is your first, and it will help you be open to receiving meaningful and helpful insights during your practice. If you have a meditation practice that works for you, great! Stick to it! In the end, do what feels right for you.

Educating yourself through reading and attending workshops and retreats is marvelous! This helps you gain the knowledge that will allow you to put things into action—but knowledge alone will only get you so far. Reading about dancing will not make you a good dancer. Making changes in your life comes with effort and action. Only when you internalize,

> **Reading about dancing will not make you a good dancer.**

experience, and integrate that knowledge into your life will you receive the benefits with lasting effects.

At some point, you simply need to start.

I understand that your life may be terrific without meditation—you eat healthy, exercise, and have loving relationships. But you don't know what you're missing. Seriously. Add regular meditation to your regimen and it will take your life to the next level!

Post-separation when I was dating Roger, life was fun and enjoyable. I enjoyed healthy eating, and I was super-active with rock-climbing, yoga, and running, but I still felt something missing in life. It's only when I dove in and did my inner work and started to get a real sense of my internal world, that life became magical. Meditation enabled me to develop an intimate relationship with the parts of me—my mind, body, feelings, and soul. And as I navigated challenges with my children and my vengeful ex-partner, I became more and more equipped to problem solve and act from a calm and centered space.

Pay attention to the parts of you that are stirring and nudging (or perhaps screaming) for your attention. When an undesirable situation arises, simply be present in your body, feel, and breathe. Doing your inner work and practicing meditation will equip you to listen to what your body and feelings are telling you.

Listen!

And then investigate!

CHAPTER 6

Investigate: Excavate the Gem

People will do anything, no matter how absurd, in order to avoid facing their own souls. One does not become enlightened by imagining figures of light, but by making the darkness conscious.

—*Carl Jung*

Are you living your happiest life?

As much as we want to be happy and live perfect lives—whether it's a loving marriage with a cute house, healthy children, and a sweet dog, or a fit and healthy body, or a prominent career, or perhaps world travel (or maybe all the above)—these don't necessarily happen.

Despite our desires, best intentions, and endless struggles at working our butts off to make our lives perfect, we find ourselves in relationships and circumstances that do not match our dreams—or our dreams appear to have manifested on the outside, but we feel lost and unhappy on the inside, or our body is weak and our health is compromised. Eventually, we justify and make excuses for the way things are, and we settle in and live in quiet desperation, waiting for our happy to happen to us.

Waiting for the kids to grow up.

Waiting for a better job.

Waiting for a vacation.

Waiting for tomorrow.

I thought I was on the road to happiness when I ended my physically abusive relationship with Nico. Little did I know that my next boyfriend was merely a new actor playing the same invasive role with a different backdrop in the movie of my life.

> **My next boyfriend was merely a new actor playing the same invasive role with a different backdrop in the movie of my life.**

I didn't *want* more abuse in my life, yet more abuse is precisely what I got.

What's up with that?

The Subconscious Mind

Here's what's up: our subconscious—a part of our autonomic nervous system that allows us to function in day-to-day life. The subconscious (*sub* meaning *below*, and *conscious* meaning *awareness*) is something of which we are not ordinarily aware but of which we can become aware if we pay attention. It differs from the unconscious (*un* meaning *without*, and *conscious* meaning *awareness*), which is something of which we cannot become aware irrespective of attention. The unconscious also functions as part of the autonomic nervous system, and it comprises our natural instincts, such as survival, while our subconscious is a creation of our environment.

Thanks to our autonomic nervous systems, our hearts beat, lungs breathe, stomachs digest, and kidneys filter. The autonomic nervous system also plays a role in functions that are not critical for life, like walking, running, driving a car, or playing an instrument. When we perform an action, neurological pathways are created that instruct the body to engage specific muscles with precise timing and with the release of certain chemicals. When we practice the activity repeatedly, the neurological pathways embed in our nervous systems, and the action becomes natural or second nature. Our nervous systems essentially create software programs that allow the steps and actions to take place automatically: we begin performing the activity without conscious effort.

The first time you learned to ride a bicycle, most (if not all) of your conscious attention was placed on pedaling and balancing. Each time you tried bicycling, your nervous system responded with the same neurological patterns. Eventually, after repeated tries, neurological pathways became fully established and memorized in your nervous system. Bicycling became an automatic subconscious program that didn't require your conscious attention.

Through the creation and automatic running of these neurological programs, the subconscious frees up our conscious attention. It's how we can talk or text while we walk, cycle, or drive. Yes, people still do this, despite the obvious dangers. And yes, I've seen people texting while cycling.

Maybe a bad example. But you get my point, right?

Our subconscious gets programmed through information that's repeated over and over—television, especially commercials, is a classic example of this. Why do you think it's called television *programming*? Advertisements leverage the programmability of the subconscious. Do you say *QTip* or cotton swab? *Kleenex* or facial tissue?

In addition to repetition, messaging that elicits a strong emotional response, such as anger, fear, love, or joy, causes programming to happen sooner and to run deeper, which means it persists for longer in our subconscious and takes more effort to bypass or deprogram.

To help understand this concept, consider how you learned the alphabet. In North America, most of us learned it through the classic *Alphabet Song*. Whoever invented this song was a genius because having kids memorize and repeat twenty-six letters would be impossible without making it fun.

The catchy tune did just that—decades later, we still know the alphabet.

Now consider what you ate for lunch two-weeks ago on this day.

Unless there was a strong emotion generated at lunch-time on that day (or, like me, you eat the same thing every weekday for lunch), chances are you won't be able to recall it.

Now, recall a time from your childhood when a caregiver or teacher yelled at you, or when a kid ridiculed or bullied you, or perhaps a time when you experienced physical trauma. Despite this incident being decades in the past, chances are you have no problem recalling details about it because of the strong emotions that were tied to it. The emotional, mental, and physical reactions embedded deeply in your subconscious.

Highly emotional events also come coupled with related beliefs. If an authority figure yelled at you or a classmate repeatedly ridiculed or bullied you when you were a child, you might have started to think that you were deserving of such behaviour, like *I'm bad, I don't fit in, I'm not smart enough,* to justify and rationalize the painful experiences and your resulting feelings. Similarly, if an authority figure praised you and your classmates adored you, you may have started to think that you were deserving of such behaviours, like *I'm good, I'm smart, I'm likable,* to justify and rationalize the plea-surable experiences and your resulting feelings.

The point is, whether accompanied with pleasure or pain, our past emotional experiences shaped our thoughts about ourselves. As children, the formation of these thoughts and subsequent beliefs was not by conscious choice—it was a func-tion and survival defense mechanism of the protective ego.

What did your caregivers or early influences tell you about yourself, your abilities, your appearance, or life in gen-eral when you were young? What emotional shock have you experienced? What beliefs about yourself, others, or life might have been formed as a result of your emotional experience?

We Become What We Believe

Most of our subconscious programs were developed early in life, often before the age of six, when we were like sponges and had no filters developed to censor the information that bombarded our receptive and absorptive minds and bodies. Our parents were great and did the best they could, but let's face it, they weren't Jesus or Buddha (and neither were their parents).

Were you told that you were "bad" or even "good"? After all, being told we were a "good girl" implied that we became good because of something we *did*, which means that if we didn't do that thing, we were "bad."

Talk about pressure on our developing psyches.

For most of us, when we were good, we were rewarded and praised and maybe hugged and kissed. And when we were bad, we were punished and we may have suffered physical, mental, or emotional consequences for our inappropriate behaviours.

So, when our early childhood influencers told us we were "bad" or "stupid" or that our opinion didn't matter because we were just a kid, we soaked it all in. And when our childhood influencers treated us poorly, with or without the words to accompany the mistreatment, we believed things about ourselves to justify the treatment. We learned that love was conditional and was based on our actions. And when we repeatedly heard or experienced things that caused us pain, emotional or otherwise, related subconscious thoughts and beliefs about ourselves and our worlds became ingrained—they essentially formed the foundational code in our software programs and comprised our baseline energy.

Subconscious programming serves us well when it's formed through lighter emotions, as in learning the *Alphabet Song*. But programming doesn't serve us well when it's created through denser emotions, as in being ridiculed and bullied by others. Without our awareness and intervention, our early subconscious programs drive our thoughts, words, and actions throughout our adult lives despite those programs being developed under conditions that no longer exist today—decades later.

Our thoughts (intentional or not) create beliefs, our beliefs shape our actions, repeated actions create habits, repeated habits create our identity or personality (personal reality), and it is through these lenses that we live and build our characters as *lazy, slacker, stupid, shy, smart, loving,* etc. Our life experiences are filtered through and created by our belief systems and identities.

Here's what this looked like in my life:

1. Repeated thought: I need to avoid anger to protect myself and stay safe.

2. Belief: Anger is wrong and leads to pain and injury.

3. Repeated action: Hide when anger arises in others and repress it and deny it when it starts rising in me.

4. Habit: Be silent. Avoid confrontation and angering people. Be agreeable and nice. Do as I'm told. Don't get angry.

5. Personality: *Mousie*—a shy and quiet girl who doesn't express her opinions or stand up for herself.

6. Life consequence: Abusive relationships and illness.

What persona(s) have you adopted? Who are you known as? The quiet one? The smart one? The dreamer? The pleaser? How has this persona affected your life? What are the consequences?

Our personal lenses or personal realities (personalities) explain how two people witnessing the same event at the same time, and at the same place, can perceive and report two entirely different stories or experiences.

I went through life unaware of my fabricated beliefs. It was only through my deep personal work that this knowledge surfaced, like my realization that I believed I was weak, small, and afraid and had been playing the role of *Mousie* throughout my entire life.

We were all born with the same capacity to realize greatness, and we have that same limitless capacity today. The only thing stopping us from experiencing it is our beliefs about ourselves. Our subconscious software programs and beliefs shape our experiences and create our realities.

Without question.

Fear not! You're not alone! We all have these subconscious programs running the show of our lives. Until they don't. Until we process the blocked energy and consciously override and reprogram our subconscious limiting beliefs with empowering ones.

The Known Path

Imagine a field covered in fresh knee-deep snow that brushes the base of the kneecaps, and that, as children, we learned from our caregivers to walk a particular path through this snow to get to the market. Through our repeated travels in the snow, the snow eventually became compacted, and a definite path formed.

As adults, we still walk the same path because it's the way we've always gone and what we've always known. The snow is firmly packed, which makes it easy and comfortable to walk on, and it's a safe route that gets us to where we want to go.

Over the years, a bridge was built that shaved thirty-minutes off the walking time to get to the market. Awesome, right?

Nope.

We keep our blinders on and continue to walk the worn-in path—the path of least resistance. We don't even realize we're missing out on an available path that would save us thirty minutes one way. We're content walking this old, established trail, but it isn't great either because it takes us an hour to get to the market, and it's kind of boring. Sometimes, we downright hate this path.

But, since this well-worn path is safe, easy, known, and comfortable, we continue to walk on it. We may catch a glimpse of the bridge in the distance, but it's scary to trudge a new path toward it. *What if it takes longer? What if it's dangerous? I don't think I can do it.* Our minds can't justify putting forth the effort of plodding through new snow, especially with unknown risks. So, we succumb to our fears and doubts, and stay stuck in the rut of the old path.

The ruts in which we walk are our subconscious beliefs and mind-made stories that keep us stuck in habitual thoughts and patterns of behaviour. These beliefs, of which we are mostly unaware, prevent us from experiencing our best life—they stop our happy from happening.

What firm, yet limiting, beliefs about yourself or life do you uphold?

It's normal to walk in these comforting ruts of life, but it's not highly functional when the grooves prevent us from seeing and considering opportunities that could lead to a fuller life and higher versions of ourselves—sooner. We settle for mediocrity, and we put up with the *devil we know.*

Great news! There is help!

Life Is a Mirror

Our very lives provide us with the necessary help to see what our subconscious is housing.

What is your world reflecting about you?

Be curious!

Our individual worlds constantly reflect our beliefs to us. If we believe we are loving, we continually encounter loving and kind people. If we think people are inherently good, we see acts of kindness, and people let us into lineups, especially when we need it most.

Similarly, if we believe we have little patience, a long lineup or a traffic jam will reflect this for us. If we think we are shy and have low confidence, social situations will make this evident. If we believe we have no power, abusive relationships will make this apparent.

I'd like to point out that we don't walk around saying, "I believe I have little patience," or "I believe I have bad luck." Instead, we utter these things in daily conversation with others, "Oh, I have no patience for that" or "I'm shy." Or we repeat it to ourselves under our breath or in our minds, *Figures. Just my luck.* Or *I'm not good enough.*

When we get emotionally activated by annoying people or distressing events, trust that there is an underlying related subconscious belief regarding some aspect of ourselves that is the root cause behind these people or events and the emotional activation arising in us. These things are there *for* us to investigate and resolve the underlying beliefs and blocked energy within.

Who annoys (or has annoyed) you and what did they do that annoyed you? What devices (blame, repressing, denying, depression, anxiety, etc.) does your ego mind use when you get annoyed?

Time and again, we repeatedly encounter these annoying people, distressing events, lineups, awkward social situations, or abusive relationships, and we fabricate stories about ourselves, others, or life in general to justify and rationalize our experiences: *I have bad luck. It's just the way I am. Life is unfair. He's a narcissist. People are always trying to take advantage of me. Money doesn't grow on trees.*

Then, we develop dysfunctional habits, like avoiding, repressing, or becoming stressed or anxious to try to mitigate or compensate for our mind's fabricated stories. The beliefs remain subconscious, the energy remains stuck, and the cycle of undesirable events perpetuates.

No one consciously *wants* aggressive people in their lives. I certainly didn't! Yet to help activate and release the heavy repressed feelings and associated beliefs from my childhood, I repeatedly found myself in abusive relationships. What better way to get my attention and stir my dormant feelings than by being beaten and abused?

But the abusive relationships didn't awaken me to the blocked feelings and stuck energy inside of me. I didn't listen to life. I had completely forgotten how to do so. So, my body joined in the efforts and created consistent low energy and repeated strep throat infections. But my mind ignored my feelings and body signals. I resolved that misery was my fate, and I pretended to be happy instead. My body then screamed in a way that I couldn't ignore and repress as I had done with my feelings and throat infections. It took a ruptured appendix to finally wake me up and truly hear what my body and life were telling me.

It was only during my personal life coaching sessions and deep introspection that I surfaced the subconscious belief that *all men are mean and scary*—precisely what the men in my life had shown me.

Aggressive men are exactly what I *needed* to wake up to the beliefs that were shaping my life and holding me back from true happiness and my life purpose. Without aggressors in my life, I wouldn't have grown to be the empowered woman I am today. I wouldn't have delved deeply into my personal work or training, and I wouldn't be writing this book and helping women shed their limiting beliefs and replace them with empowering ones.

Authors need beta readers and editors because we are blind to our own mistakes. Likewise, we usually cannot see our subconscious limiting beliefs, so life faithfully shows these to us through the people and circumstances in our lives that act as our trusted *editors*.

Life shows us what we need to see within ourselves, so we can release it and grow.

The mirror reflects things as they are, it doesn't reflect what we *want* or *hope* to see. If we don't like how our hair looks in the mirror, we can't fix our hair by adjusting our reflection in the mirror, right?

We must adjust our *inner selves* to change what we don't like in the mirror.

No exceptions.

What belief would you need to let go of to simply allow your annoyances to be as they are

> **We must adjust our *inner selves* to change what we don't like in the mirror.**

without affecting your emotional state and energy? What would the consequence be if you let go of that belief?

Our growth and self-mastery are the only things going on in this project in which we've so courageously embarked. We are capable of miracles beyond our minds' comprehension, and our lives, as mirrors of our internal terrain, are the means through which we are empowered to gain our self-mastery.

Life, even and especially the undesirable aspects, is continually happening for our growth. And the longer we refuse to listen and investigate what life is revealing to us, the more unignorable the life events will become.

It's important not to speculate about what we *think* we need to learn because this may do more harm than good. Remember, the protective ego mind will rationalize (*rational lies)*, so the less we get our thinking minds involved, the better!

Go straight to the source: your body—it never lies!

Take a moment and reflect on the undesirable people, conditions, or things in your life—the ones you stew about. If thoughts of these people, circumstances, or things stir a feeling of discomfort in you, then realize that there is a subconscious belief preventing you from realizing and owning a higher aspect of yourself. These people, circumstances, or things are there to reflect stuck energy and limiting beliefs within you that need to be released.

Similarly, your body's symptoms and ailments reflect this blocked energy that is begging for your attention and release, just as my persistent strep throat infections were intended for me to pay attention inwardly to find and use my voice and stand up for myself.

We Requested It

No one willingly makes themselves unhappy. So, when we're feeling unhappy, our egos naturally deflect and look to blame people, conditions, or things to justify our unhappiness. *I'm grumpy because... my teen was vile this morning. I had a terrible sleep. My back is aching. My house flooded this morning. It's raining. It's too hot. It's too cold.* Fill in the blank: _____.

Blaming external factors and being a victim of people, places, conditions, or things is a normal part of the ego's defense system. It's the ego's job. Blaming is a natural and perfectly logical reaction that helps us feel good—initially and momentarily—but it keeps us from owning our issues and stepping into our personal power. When we externalize, point blame at others, or play victim to others or our circumstances, we give our power to create change away. In the end, this leads to undesirable or downright awful patterns in our lives.

Similarly, we can blame ourselves and get into the *should haves* and become a victim to our judgmental minds. We'll cover this in the next chapter.

We all have annoyances in life, big and small, that we can tolerate to some degree. A bit of a radical idea here (heads-up ego). If we can acknowledge that these annoyances are happening *for* us and that our souls requested them for us to grow, then we become empowered to make changes that prevent them, or similar experiences, from happening again.

Wait. What?

Let me say this again.

If we can acknowledge that an undesirable event is happening *for* us and that our souls requested it for us to grow, then we become empowered to make changes that prevent it, or similar experiences, from happening again.

Stop and notice any resistance you feel after reading this concept!

What do you feel in your body as you reflect on the circumstances which annoy you and entertain the idea that your soul asked for it?

Now ponder this: what do you stand to lose by entertaining the idea that maybe, just maybe, your soul requested the situation or circumstance, as lousy and terrible as it feels? Especially if it meant that seeing things this way would result in greater ease and happiness for you?

Know that resisting this idea is perfectly normal!

I certainly resisted it for most of my life.

Now what if you expand this concept beyond annoyances to weightier circumstances in life? Perhaps your soul chose your abusive partner so that you could find your strength, declare your truth, speak up, and stand up for yourself.

How else could you learn these powerful qualities without the classroom in which to learn them?

How do we learn patience without a line up?

If we can accept and admit to ourselves that, at the soul level, we created this mess, then we gain the power and authority to dis-create it. We become empowered to create change by taking ownership and accountability.

> **We become empowered to create change by taking ownership and accountability.**

What painful event in your life has happened that your mind has judged as bad? What gifts could you possibly gain if you pretended that your soul requested it?

To experience your happy now, it's crucial that you get curious, investigate, and adjust inwardly rather than point blame, become a victim, deflect feelings, or try to control things outwardly. The people, conditions, or things that aggravate you are there *for you* as your mirror to help you see your limiting thoughts which you can't otherwise see, so you can move through the blocks and grow into a higher version of yourself.

My friend, the people in your life who annoy you are simply your editors.

No buts.

They're simply messengers who are revealing parts of yourself that hold blocked energy that you otherwise would be blind to.

Yes, some experiences and life events really suck. I get it.

Without these aggravating challenges being a mirror for you, you would remain blind to your self-imposed transparent limitations and the blocked energy behind them. These opportunities, which at the time feel like anything but an opportunity, provide you with a starting point to become inwardly aware of that which needs to change within yourself, so you can override and rewrite your dysfunctional software programs.

Override Your Dysfunctional Programming

Marriages dissolve. Children grow up and leave. Companies lay off. Loved ones pass on. Friends get busy.

What is the one thing that will never, ever leave you?

Your breath!

Breathing is the one subconscious function which we can consciously regulate to override our subconscious reactions and stop the cascade of neurological sequences of our software programs. The deep, rhythmic breathing of which we learned in the previous chapter, calms the nervous system and switches it from fight-or-flight to rest-and-digest mode.

When I finally started meditating and wanted to make it a way of life, I practiced it daily, like any learned skill that I wanted to be fluent at. With repeated practice, a subconscious program was created that ran automatically when I felt stress approaching. I was able to rely on my developed meditation skills to create feelings of ease and love within me—stress dissolved despite the world spinning outside of me.

A committed practice of meditation is like taking blinders off that are preventing you from seeing that time-saving bridge through the deep snow. It will open unlimited possibilities in your life!

Do not wait for an emotional trigger to begin using your breath as a tool because you'll quickly get discouraged. Develop the skill ahead of time. Deep breathing and meditation are crucial tools in your LIFE Method™.

Build on the Foundation of Meditation

In the last chapter, we reviewed some fundamental aspects of meditation, and doing just those basics regularly will improve your life. I'm recommending an expanded practice here to build on the foundation and enhance the effects.

In the steps that follow, I suggest visualizing light. Colour is perceived by us through our senses according to the frequency at which it resonates: lighter colours have higher frequencies while darker colours are denser and have lower frequencies. Considering we are composed of energy, we want to expose our bodies to high frequency energy as often as possible to promote the resonance of lighter feelings in our bodies. Energy is contagious and the synchronizing of ticking of clocks in the same room proves this phenomenon. The same is true of sound and light waves: listening to inspirational/classical music and exposing ourselves to high frequency light literally shifts our energy to higher frequencies that feel good in the body.

I also suggest generating a feeling of love in your body during meditation, and the means to do so was explained in Chapter Five. But consider making this a habit that you do not only during meditation, but throughout your day! The more often we can experience ourselves as the feeling of love, the more our energetic blueprint will take on that vibration. The feeling of love is the highest frequency we can feel in our bodies, and it's a great vibe to be riding!

Who doesn't want to feel the warm and fuzzy feelings of love all day?

A quieted mind coupled with deep belly breaths, visualization of light, and the feeling of love is a powerful combination that will transform your life!

1. Start by giving yourself permission to experience whatever arises during your time with yourself—thoughts, feelings, and all.

2. During your sacred special time alone, simply breathe deeply and rhythmically and observe where your mind goes. Get to know your thoughts. When you notice a thought, simply acknowledge it, *oh look, there's a thought,* and then bring your attention back to the breath. Slow, steady, and deep breathing. In and out through the nose.

3. While focusing the mind on the breath, imagine your breath as a floating brilliant white sphere of light. On the inhale, it moves from above your head in through your crown, the center of your head, along your spine, and then into your heart. On the exhale, your breath (as this dazzling white light) moves down along your spine and through your tailbone to beneath where you sit or stand. Remember, deep belly breaths throughout.

4. Reverse the path. Inhale this glowing sphere from below where you sit up toward the heart and then exhale from the heart to above the crown of your head.

5. Generate a feeling of love in your body and continue with your breathwork while experiencing this feeling of love.

If you are drawn to a certain colour, play with visualizing it in your mind's eye and your body during your practice. The appearance of this colour coming into your awareness is there for a reason. So, go with it, and add it to your practice! You'll find that other colours will eventually arise. Each has a frequency that corresponds to a level of conscious awareness located at various centers in your body. Not coincidentally, the colours correspond to those of the rainbow.

Use your imagination. Let it feel good and enjoyable.

Ten minutes a day. You can do this!

Discharge Your Reactive Energy

But what about those moments when you feel like you're going to scream, hit someone, or throw something, and your meditation practice isn't fully developed? Not exactly a moment for breathing with light and love, right?

Yeah. I know.

The following exercise helped me discharge activated energy when Zeydan was hovering over me and screaming "fuck off" at the top of his lungs. In the instances where you feel like you're about to lose it, the goal is to diffuse the bomb before someone gets hurt and your learning opportunity is blown up... which will mean that you can expect a similar scene, with or without the same actors, to appear for a second, third, or hundredth time for another chance at your self-mastery.

1. The moment you get activated, diffuse the emotional charge in your body with an immediate and aggressive exhale through the mouth. Even if there's nothing left in the lungs—exhale. Completely.

2. Where possible, remove yourself from the situation. Resist your ego's urge to snap back and defend yourself. Just walk away.

3. Sit or stand with a straight spine, and let the next inhale be through the nose. It should be deep and slow. Your belly should expand fully. Visualize white light coming in as you do this.

4. Let the exhale be assertive and through the mouth, and visualize heavy dark clouds of energy being released through your mouth or belly button, whichever feels intuitively right for you.

5. Repeat this style of breathing for a few cycles until the strong energy charge is diffused. You'll feel when this happens.

After the feeling that you want to scream or punch something or someone has passed, it's time to do some subtler work. This would be the starting point for a mild annoyance as well.

1. Remind yourself that, at some level, you needed this to see a new part of yourself that you are ready to learn about, experience, and grow into; otherwise, it wouldn't be happening.

2. Be your own best friend. Tell yourself that it's normal for you to feel this way because anyone who's been through what you've been through or just experienced would feel this way! Let it be okay to have these feelings because it *is* okay! Remember, feelings aren't good, bad, right, or wrong, they're simply feelings—communication from your Higher Self to keep you aligned with the paved path.

3. Then, immediately assert to yourself that it's not functional for you to be feeling this way because you are a mature, capable, and empowered adult who doesn't need ego defenses to feel safe.

4. Do a body scan and notice the part of your body that was activated with the event. Find where there is discomfort—perhaps a tightness, or a stinging, burning, aching, or pulsing sensation. This is your body talk. Listen to it. Investigate it!

5. Squeeze the area in your body that's talking to you: let it know you're listening! Apply pressure with your

hands from the outside and squeeze the muscles from the inside.

6. Now breathe. Back straight. In through the nose and deep into the belly, so it expands. As you breathe in, visualize bright white light coming in from above the crown of your head, travelling along your spine to your heart and the space that was activated. Breathe right through the activated area.

7. As you exhale, visualize this light moving down your spine and out through your tailbone into the earth below you.

8. Then reverse the path of the light and breathe in and up through your tailbone, to the activated space and your heart, and then exhale out the top of your head.

Use your imagination here! Visualization works because the mind cannot tell real from imagined. Be patient, tender, and loving with yourself as you do this breathwork.

Fear Is Your Compass

As you continue to investigate, use life as your mirror, and work with your body and your breath when growth opportunities arise (as they certainly will), you'll begin to develop an intimate and trusting relationship with yourself. You'll refine your ability to feel and sense your gut feelings, and you'll eventually learn to follow them.

But be forewarned: your intuition will likely lead you to make decisions that veer from the deeply engrained path that you have been walking for years or decades. Plodding a new path in deep snow will take more effort than walking on a path of compacted snow—in fact, it may downright suck initially! It takes courage to try something new, and new things can feel scary! Have faith and believe that although this may be tough right now, it will be more comfortable in the end. The rewards are well worth the effort.

What do you desire in life that fear is stopping you from pursuing?

Rest assured that the feeling of fear is a wonderful sign that you're heading into growth—and despite the uncomfortable sensations that may arise with it, fear is the doorway through which you head toward the paved path.

When you observe and allow fear and move into it, rather than away from it, you step into unlimited potential where a new version of you exists—the version that goes beyond your antiquated limiting beliefs and habits which were formed as a child or young adult but which no longer serve you as a mature and functional adult today.

When Asia, my daughter, was two, I contemplated leaving my abusive relationship with Seth. And oh my, the fear was unbearable for me at the time. I wasn't stable in my knowledge and application of the tools and practices that I have in place today, so the awful feeling of fear and the *what-ifs* stopped me from taking action and leaving Seth.

The result?

I lived in misery for another *eight* years. If, when fear first arose, I had regarded it as an opportunity for growth and stepped into it, the discomfort of fear would have lasted roughly a month.

A month versus eight years of discomfort?

Hmm.

Thankfully, my ruptured appendix spoke far louder than the fear-based stories my mind was generating. I mean, what would be the next sign if a ruptured appendix didn't work? A crippling car accident? Fatal disease? I became quiet enough long enough to sense and feel my truth at a deep, undeniable level. I knew that separating was the right decision. I believed and trusted my intuition and took a leap of faith into fear.

The ego mind will resist fear and discomfort by attempting to control our external environment and keep things in the known. Simply trust that it's far easier to allow the feelings of fear for a short time than it is to endure years of struggle and repeated lessons by resisting it.

Note that danger is different than fear. Fear (FEAR: False Evidence Appearing Real), is a perception of the mind. It's imagined. And deep breaths and a refocused mind will prove it. Danger, on the other hand, is real in that it can cause harm, physical, mental, emotional, or otherwise. If you're in danger, what I'm saying here does not apply! In that case, follow your protective instinct, assert your boundaries if necessary, and flee—or whatever it is you need to do to get to safety.

Expect fear to arise, and when it does, welcome it and talk to your protective mind. Assure yourself that you've got this and that it's normal to be scared and that everything will be perfectly okay. Then breathe in the way described earlier. The deep breaths will help to override the mind's reactive and protective state. Consider fear as your compass that points you in the direction of desired growth and be open to learning something new.

When we avoid learning and trying new things, we stunt our growth and expansion into the fullness of ourselves. A fruit is either green and growing or it's ripe and rotting.

> **Choose fear over the comfort of the known. You'll look back and wish you would have taken that step into fear a lot sooner.**

Please don't rot.

Consider a fear that is stopping you from taking action. What would life look like if you didn't have that fear?

Why not be proactive and purposely make decisions that elicit some sense of fear in you?

Get curious about fear! Embrace it and step through it. Explore the other side of it where you'll discover a more empowered version of you.

Go ahead!

Choose fear over the comfort of the known. You'll look back and wish you would have taken that step into fear a lot sooner.

With these foundational practices in your toolbox, you'll begin to meet challenges in your Project: LIFE with ammunition and ability. When you get emotionally or physically activated, resist the urge to defend, combat, and blame. Call upon your meditation tools and go within. You'll interrupt the nuclear chain reaction that would otherwise kick in along with the dysfunctional programming that would create the same-old undesirable outcome again and again. Instead, you'll create a new result, a brighter future, and an elevated version of you.

As you continue using life as your mirror and investigating your internal terrain, memories of old circumstances and past hurts may arise that will need extra attention and loving care from you. Forgiveness is a vital tool to help move you through this next phase of your LIFE Method™.

CHAPTER 7

Forgive: Free Yourself from the Past

When one door of happiness closes, another opens; but often we look so long at the closed door that we do not see the one that has opened for us.

—*Helen Keller*

I couldn't decide whether to make this chapter about forgiveness or fun, as both are important and start with an *f.*

Our analytical ego minds classify things as black or white, up or down, when the answer is often *both*. We experience our physical worlds according to the contrast created between these oppositional dyads. In the spiritual world, however, there are only triads, and all possibilities exist at once. The more we embrace *both/and* in our lives rather than *either/or*, the more we attune to our spiritual world and live as our Higher Selves in physical form.

I'm including *both* forgiveness and fun because each is an essential component in experiencing happiness in our lives.

It has nothing to do with the indecisive aspect of my personality.

Ahem.

Let's start with the more seemingly solemn of the two.

Forgive

I have yet to meet someone who has not had at least one traumatic experience in their life, to some degree, either physical, mental, or emotional.

As a child, were you spanked? Were you yelled at? Were you punished in some form or another? Were you reprimanded by a teacher, a boss, or a partner?

If you think you don't have anyone to forgive, think again. Because chances are you were negatively impacted at some point in your life, and you have some unresolved energy from it.

Most significant traumas occurred early in our childhood by a parent, another family member, a caretaker, or a person of authority. These early traumas affected our entire lives through repressed energy and the subsequent subconscious beliefs that were formed.

Keep in mind that events that caused great upset may have been buried deeply and forgotten altogether, in which case, we'll be unaware of any past upsets or trauma. Burying memories and painful events is a protective mechanism of the mind—it was like anesthesia for our psyches that helped us function and survive at the time those traumas occurred. But burying and forgetting about painful events does not rid the heavy emotional energy of them from our subconscious.

Simply be on the lookout with full emotional disclosure—is your mind minimizing any past traumas that emotionally impacted you?

Regardless of whether we are knowingly or unknowingly harbouring regret, resentment, bitterness, anger, or shame, the energy of these feelings is heavy—it literally weighs us down, and, over time, creates discomfort and dis-ease in our bodies and lives. When we hold on to resentment, the energy of it comprises our baseline energy, and our level of happiness in life will only be as great as the energy from the heaviest emotion that remains buried within.

At this moment, your mind is likely thinking, *I'm not holding onto any heavy emotions.*

My friend. Welcome to the rational lies of the ego.

Don't worry, though. It's normal. Everyone's ego automatically minimizes past hurts to avoid feeling hurt in the present moment.

It's not until we change our energy that we can create our dream lives because we attract what we are (and what we need to heal), not what we *want.*

So, how do we change our energy?

Aside from the breathing practices already covered, this is where forgiveness comes in.

The Unforgivable

What about unmentionable horrific acts of intrusion? How can these possibly be forgiven, especially if we were helpless and innocent small children?

At some point in our lives, we learned that holding a grudge and not forgiving another person somehow gets back at them. We feel we get even by not forgiving, and with that, we feel a sense of retribution.

I will never forgive him for that.
Sound familiar?

Or perhaps we believe that forgiving the perpetrator means

> **Forgiveness is the doorway to freedom from your past.**

we're sending them or others a message that what they did was okay when it was anything but.

Forgiveness is the doorway to freedom from your past.

When you hang on to bitterness or resentment, or you hold a grudge and feel done wrong by, you remain emotionally, mentally, and energetically bound to the perpetrator. Imagine a rope tied around your waist that binds you to that person, and through that rope, you give your valuable energy to the other—this is essentially what's happening.

Who do you need to forgive?

Always go with the first name that pops into your awareness.

You leak energy and lose power by hanging on to resentment.

To help illustrate the logic behind this, imagine the following scene. Visualize yourself walking to the fridge. You stop and open the door and dig for a lemon. After finding a deep yellow lemon, you place it on a cutting board. You pull out a sharp knife from the drawer and slice the lemon into quarters as it squirts cold juice on your hands and the counter. You put down the knife, grab a wedge, smell the pungent and tart aroma, and bite into it.

If you haven't done so, yet, take a moment, close your eyes, and visualize the scene and biting into that lemon.

Did your mouth start to salivate?

While under hypnosis, people who are merely *told* that they're getting burned by a cigarette develop lesions on their skin as though an actual cigarette had burned them. Whether you know what your mind is saying or not, and whether what your mind is saying is true, false, real, or imagined, your body will respond.

So, not only does the baseline energy of resentment affect your level of happiness, but each time you stew about, complain, or simply recall the event, you're basically making yourself sick. When you recall a past "unforgivable" event, the cascade of chemical reactions that you experienced at the time of the event occurs in the present. Similar to how your mouth reacted to you visualizing biting into a lemon, your mind and body experience the trauma of the past as though it were happening in the present.

Holding a grudge against the perpetrator has no impact on their lives.

Zero.

Zilch.

The only person your resentment negatively affects is *you*, and perhaps your loved ones.

Forgiveness does not mean you're letting the perpetrator "off the hook" or that you're doing *them* a favour... because you're *not*.

Forgiveness does *not* mean that you agree with what happened.

This is important! Allow your definition of forgiveness to realign here.

Forgiveness simply means that you're no longer willing to allow the perpetrator or event to have a toxic influence in your life today. Forgiveness allows you to reclaim the energy and power that you have lost from holding onto past hurts.

Forgiveness is self-protection. It's something you do for *you*—not them. Not anyone. Just *you*.

By choosing to not forgive, you are choosing to hold on to resentment, bitterness, etc. What will you gain by holding on to these lower emotions?

If you've had an old-school definition of forgiveness in your mind, perhaps it's time to let that go and give it an upgrade.

Perhaps (hint, hint) you want to assure your mind and repeat after me: *Forgiveness is for my self-protection. Forgiveness frees me from the toxic energy of my past.*

It's silly, yes! But it works.

Try it a second time and with a little more oomph! Because, remember, what we experience with emotion sticks in our subconscious.

So, we know *why* we forgive and *what* it means. What about *how?*

How to Forgive

How do we free ourselves from the toxic influence of past hurts?

Our minds are hard-wired to repress, minimize, and deny painful aspects of our lives to protect us from experiencing pain (physical, mental, emotional, or otherwise). To forgive and release ourselves from the toxic influence of the past, we first need to acknowledge that what happened actually happened.

When I first studied forgiveness as part of my training, my ego's defensive self-talk started immediately, *Pfft, I don't need this exercise. I had a happy childhood. Nico and Seth weren't really that bad... they could have been worse.*

Seriously, though. What child wouldn't be impacted by seeing bullet holes in their parents' dresser and being chased by her angry stepdad? What girl wouldn't be scared stiff by being punched by her aggressive boyfriend? My protective ego hid these truths and denied them all, and thus, I thought I had nothing to forgive. My ego minimized and rejected the truth of what I experienced in the past to prevent me from feeling emotional pain in the present.

I could only heal and release the repressed energy from my past upsets by first admitting to myself that what happened actually happened. Admitting things happened doesn't mean we're saying it was our fault—because it wasn't. But it *is* our responsibility to heal because no one else is going to do it for us. Acknowledging what happened simply means that we're ready to see it as it truly was so that we can free ourselves from it. We simply need to admit to ourselves that there is something to actually be forgiven.

Despite my ego's resistance, I completed the forgiveness exercises during my life coaching training. And with that, I experienced a release of emotions that had been bogged down for decades. I facilitate this powerful exercise with my coaching students, and the response is unanimous—people feel lighter and at peace after.

I'm not saying that forgiveness is going to change your life radically in an instant (although it may). It's simply one of many holistic tools to help things shift, get energy flowing, and get life moving in more desirable (and functional) ways.

Forgiving trespassers is a deeply emotional and involved exercise that I facilitate with my students. Without getting into the depths of our pain here, suffice it to say that you begin to cultivate an environment within yourself to let go of the past and release the stuck energy of resentment through the following condensed forgiveness activity.

1. Genuinely understand *why* you want to forgive.

2. State your intention to forgive and release the past for your personal health and wellbeing.

3. List all the things that your trespasser did to hurt you. List all their traits that you can't stand. What did you loathe about them and what they did? Get it all out and onto that paper until nothing about that person or event remains hidden inside of you.

4. Read the list aloud and allow your feelings to flow.

5. Breathe in the manner described earlier to process and release your feelings.

6. State your intention to forgive your trespasser, completely and unconditionally, and that you're doing so for your protection and wellbeing. If you feel safe enough doing so, visualize them and tell them this to their face in your vision.

7. When you feel complete, dispose of the list in an untraceable manner. With this, you dispose of any residual toxic energy that may have been left behind.

8. Wash your hands to symbolize the removal of any traces of toxicity from that past event.

9. Elevate your energy by immersing yourself in nature or by listening, singing, or dancing to uplifting music. When all else fails, do jumping jacks.

We Are Our Own Worst Enemies

Now that we've covered the obvious—forgiving others—what about forgiving ourselves? Not only do our rampant negative and sabotaging thoughts limit us and create our undesirable experiences and reality, but we rehash and stew over our past *should-haves* and *shouldn't-haves* and keep our energy stuck in a heavy state.

Was it my choice to remain in an abusive relationship?

Yes.

Did it suck?

Yes.

Do I wish that I would have created a safer home for me and my children?

Yes.

Should I have left the abusive relationship sooner?

?

There is no answer, because there are no *should haves*.

What's done is done. The past is behind us. If it was not meant to be, it would not be. In fact, it was precisely what was needed for all involved.

Take a moment and simply notice your body sensations. How do you feel after reading that? Did any feelings of unease arise? If so, know that it's normal, and give yourself permission to feel resistance.

Trusting that there is a purpose in all things—exactly as they are—is likely a new concept to your belief system which your ego will likely reject. We've been led to believe otherwise our entire lives along with judging things as good or bad. And if something is bad, how could it be what was needed, right?

A few years ago, my car was rear-ended in traffic. As the woman and I exchanged insurance information, we were amused to discover that our children were in the same grade at the same school. A few months later at an entrepreneurial workshop, this same woman sat at my table. We laughed at the uncanny coincidence and shared a little about ourselves and what we did for a living. I shared my life story, and I beamed as I expressed the unconditional love that I experienced every day and how I guided my students to cultivate the same within themselves. Something within the woman twinged as she heard this.

Almost two years later, this woman approached me and became my life coaching student. And after just ten weeks, she began to feel love and compassion for herself, for the first time in her life.

Now, answer this: was the collision a bad thing?

Surely, the woman felt it was a disaster at the time, and that she *should have* paid more attention and driven slower, but her soul knew better! In fact, her soul arranged it, and it was perfect and exactly what was needed for her personal growth. Thankfully, it only took two years for her to realize the blessing in that seemingly bad situation.

Life knows what it's doing! Our minds have only a glimpse of a portion of the puzzle—our souls have the box with the picture of the puzzle on it. Trust that even the bad things have a purpose. Have patience and allow the gift and blessing to reveal itself.

Stop shoulding on yourself!

What feels awful today is indeed a gift for all souls involved, we just don't consciously realize it until some point in the future. And the bigger the catastrophe and upset, the greater the gift and growth. Entertain the idea that the things in the past that you beat yourself up over were needed precisely at the time that they occurred.

If you want to change your energy and be happy, forgiving yourself for the things you are rehashing and regretting must be a part of your wellness routine to free up that energy and create space for love.

Take action! Free yourself from your own self-sabotaging thoughts.

1. Shift to an empowering mindset on your past "wrongdoings." Post little notes in your spaces. Create a note on your phone or set an hourly alarm and name it, "If it was not meant to be, it would not be" or something similar like, "I may not see it now, but the miracle will become obvious." Keep bombarding your subconscious mind with statements of faith, hope, and trust that a divine plan is in place and it's for a cause that is far greater than your mind can foresee along with its small desires and limited judgments of good and bad.

2. During your breathwork practices, visualize a violet flame surrounding you. Violet is a high frequency colour that has transmuting and cleansing qualities. Allow it to transmute any feelings of guilt, doubt, shame, and unworthiness. Do this regularly, and you'll release the energy associated with those heavier feelings. You'll feel lighter and be able to let go of the things of your past that don't serve you today.

Now that the serious stuff is behind us, let's get to the fun stuff.

We don't stop playing because we grow old; we grow old because we stop playing.

—*George Bernard Shaw*

Have Fun

Strangely enough, being fun and having fun can be more difficult than it sounds, and, well, be not so fun.

Look at young children today—not the ones entranced by their electronics, the other ones. They're always smiling, giggling, and playing, right?

One could reasonably assume that having fun is a natural thing. But considering most of us don't walk around smiling and laughing all day, one could also reasonably assume that somewhere along the way, we learned that life was tough and that we needed to be serious.

How many times a day do you enjoy a good laugh?

I was raised by a hard-working German mom and an angry Hungarian stepdad.

Work first, play later.

Not only did I forget how to laugh in life, but I also forgot how to play! My ego got addicted to working. Instead of playtime with the kids after dinner, I insisted that homework be completed first. And after homework, I needed to get work done around the house, like prep lunches, tend to the pets, clean the house, do laundry, and put away toys. The list went on. And only after I tackled some of the things on this endless list of chores, did I feel satisfied and ready to spend quality time with the kids, which ended up being only a short while before it was time to get to work again and get the kids ready for bed.

I couldn't breathe easy and relax until work was finished. It's just the way I was and thought I needed to be because it's all I knew based on my upbringing and what I believed. It was the "right" way and the only way I knew at the time.

But there's always work to be done. So, when is it okay to relax and enjoy ourselves?

It wasn't until I decided to be happy, with or without Seth, that I consciously chose to make playing with the kids a priority for me. At first, I simply went through the motions of playing—I was being fun for the kids. But with vigilance and persistence, I overcame my habitual tendency to work instead of play, and I got the hang of the fun thing. I learned to loosen up. I learned to be uninhibited, silly, and goofy. I learned how to play like a kid again and started to have fun. I got absorbed in the moment of play and enjoyed myself and my playtime with the kids.

Why can't we go about our days *and* have fun? I mean, why can't we just have fun at any given moment? What's preventing us from doing this?

I get it, some environments are simply not fun—like some relationships in my past. And if you find yourself in an anti-fun climate, then take a good look in the mirror and see what subconscious beliefs are creating that reality for you and keeping you stuck in it.

But, in any environment, being happy is a choice. It's a mindset, which you can achieve with proven steps to get you there.

Today, being playful and having fun is just the way I am because I've reprogrammed my subconscious beliefs and have changed my energy. There isn't a day that goes by where I don't have several full-hearted belly laughs. I play and have fun for me, and everyone around me benefits from it. It's contagious.

Victim No More

This collective project of LIFE is continually providing us with a practice ground to test our skills of higher living. My hormonal and moody fifteen-year-old daughter provides me with opportunities for ample practice. In the moments where she's so grumpy that words only come out as deep, mumbled grunts as she refuses to go to school or take care of her responsibilities around the home, I get to apply my tools and practice being the highest version of myself.

The keyword above is *opportunities*.

Life is continuously happening for us. Yes, the insensitive and abusive spouses, the unsupportive and brash bosses, and even the grumpy and defiant teens, they are all there *for* us as our editors.

Everyone feels justified and right according to their perspectives and the stories running in their minds. Despite what our egos may try to tell us, no one is purposely "out to get us." The other is merely behaving in a way that feels right from their own viewpoint. They, too, are learning their own lessons in life. Without question, everyone is doing the best they can given their past experiences, current circumstances, and their subsequent thoughts and beliefs, known or unknown, about themselves and life. Everyone is wearing their own lenses that colour their experiences and actions. Just because their lenses are grey while ours are purple doesn't make the other bad or wrong.

The moment we take things personally and believe that someone is doing something to intentionally get back at us or piss us off, we become a victim and we lose our ability to take charge of the situation and our response to it. It puts us into a reactive mode rather than a creative mode. When we are in creative mode, we get to choose our thoughts and feelings and our response to events—and there is no limit on this. Why not choose thoughts that feel good in your body? By intentionally selecting a higher thought or feeling, you shift your energy and transform the situation in a way that is favourable for all involved.

What about the challenges we encounter in life that feel utterly crappy?

This is where unattachment is of great benefit.

Unattachment

Unattachment helps keep us from losing our minds in situations that test our limits, belief systems, and coping strategies.

By *unattachment,* I'm not saying don't give a crap. Unlike *detachment,* which often involves a dissociation of feelings, I'm suggesting the contrary: care enough to remain stable in your emotions so you can respond from a grounded and centered state and come from a place of love, as opposed to a place of emotional immaturity and defensive reactivity that simply fuels the fire of a situation. Our subconscious reactions exacerbate the so-called problem and keep similar problems returning until we learn the lesson and realize a higher quality within ourselves.

Some movies are so captivating that you forget you're watching a movie: you get sucked into it. You feel the feelings the actors are portraying. You get tense, excited, scared, happy, and mad, or you may laugh or cry. But when the movie ends, you snap out of it and realize, *oh, right, back to reality,* and you move along in your life leaving the drama and emotions behind.

Life is a movie.

We can choose to observe it and not get sucked into the drama of it, or we can become emotionally involved and attached and be the actor and experience all the feelings and emotions in the drama—which is great when life goes according to our devised plans. But when life goes according to a grander script that we didn't sign up for, it kind of sucks being the actor.

The ego plays the actor and gets caught up in the drama. You are the one watching the movie (actually, you're directing the movie and, in fact, are the light shining through the projector, but that's a different book). At any given moment, with the assistance of the breathwork and the key principles already covered, you can be the observer of what's going on in your life. And when you do so, life begins to get easier.

Watch the movie, don't get sucked into it.

With this witness-observer practice, things outside of you can change while you remain centered and grounded and observe the show. It means that your sense of self doesn't fluctuate depending on people or things outside of you, whether it be the defiant teen, grumpy spouse, unreasonable boss, or a cold and rainy day.

> **Watch the movie, don't get sucked into it.**

Pay attention the next time someone close to you is angry or upset and notice if their words, actions, or emotional state affect your emotional state. If your child or partner is angry and complaining, do you start to get annoyed and grumpy?

It's normal that we become enmeshed and attached to conditions outside of ourselves and to those who are closest to us. It's not a bad thing, it's just not functional, especially if you have a teen, a spouse, a job, or live anywhere other than Hawaii.

Our minds will resist *what is* when people, conditions, or things don't conform to our mind's idea of what they *should* be. And when the ego mind can't fit *what is* into its limited paradigm of knowns, it kind of freaks out because it doesn't know what to expect or how to react in these new conditions to ensure our loved ones, and ourselves, are safe according to that which constitutes normalcy and safety for us.

I was devasted and depressed after the rude awakening of my son's birth. My mind was so attached to *my* plan of his birth and the way *I* was going to parent him as a newborn, that I was blindly willing to risk his life for it.

Insert name calling and judgments here: _____.

This is a hefty example of how our minds' attachments to our wants is not healthy or functional.

What in your life isn't going the way you had hoped? Your career? Relationships? Health? The way your kids behave? The way your partner behaves? Are your attachments to the way you wanted things to be causing you or others distress?

When we have a solid foundation and a firmly rooted sense of our Higher Self, we can unattach from our ideals and others and remain in a higher emotional state to better function in life and support our loved ones. Our own mental and emotional health is the greatest gift we can give to ourselves and our loved ones.

By staying empowered in our lighter energy despite another's heavy emotions, we are like a beacon of light shining forth to guide them back to their own stable and grounded state.

As much as our egos would like to control things outside of us, including our loved ones, even for their own safety and wellbeing, we need to understand that our parents, partners, and young adult children are their own people entitled to make their own choices, be the way they want to be, and experience the natural consequences of their decisions and actions—all in the name of growth.

In extreme cases, a parent can become so attached to their idea of how their child should behave that when their child does not act in a way that jives with their vision, they disown the child because the pain of separating from the child is easier to endure than the pain of letting go of their attachment to how they think their child should behave. Instead of accepting the child's behaviour as it is, they disassociate from the child and from the part of themselves that loves the child. It's merely an ego strategy to avoid the lesser of two pains. Again, it's a normal response, but it's not functional (or kind for that matter).

Eventually, the repressed pain and blocked emotions from disassociation beg for our attention and release. The amount of inner turmoil and subsequent addictions and illness eventually consume our lives.

To whom are you attached? Whose mood and behaviours affect your energy? If you let go of the mental and emotional attachments to that person, what would you lose?

The lack of energy and frequent illness I experienced throughout my relationship with Seth was a natural consequence of disassociating from him and from the many uncomfortable feelings that attempted to surface within me. I separated from the part of myself that was feeling emotional pain when I simply needed to see the feelings as they were and release them—perhaps scream and cry, or, at the least, talk to a professional about it.

No one should have to suffer and experience physical discomfort. When we see our feelings, accept them as they are, and release them, the energy of them moves and we're left feeling lighter, healthier, and happier. It's ten minutes of discomfort to spare a lifetime of suffering.

Shunning our responsibilities or ignoring the people that don't conform to our ideas and wishes is called denial and disassociation. It not only disassociates others from ourselves, but it also disassociates parts of ourselves from our awareness—the result is despair, depression, or disease. The dense energy of the denied emotions remains bound within us and affects our ability to create a happy life.

Wait.

We're supposed to be talking about fun in this section, right?

It gets better! There's hope and a way!

Unattached Involvement

We can't control the forces of nature or the actions of others. So, when life happens or our loved ones behave in a way that shatters our belief systems and expectations, it's best (for all involved) for us to process our feelings in a healthy way. In the same breath, we accept that which is before us and we engage in a compassionate manner, providing support for our loved one, rather than disassociating from them and from parts of ourselves.

Unattached involvement provides us with saving grace, especially in difficult circumstances. Unattachment ensures that we remain stable in who we are so that we can observe life (and others and their choices) without our mental and emotional states fluctuating. But, in the same breath, we remain involved as active participants because we care.

You're probably not reading this sitting in solitude in a cave in India, so you likely need to be functioning in your world and actively participating in it and the lives of others. But participate without getting sucked into the emotional drama. Simply *watch* the movie *and* provide assistance where it's needed.

It was this same skill that allowed me to be genuinely amused when the Culligan Man walked into my home as I stood in the kitchen with the police officer, the mental health nurse, and my son frying eggs. I became able to laugh at life and be entertained by it. I merely watched the show and took part as an emotionally grounded and unattached observer, rather than an emotionally enmeshed actor.

Keep the reactive ego at bay. Be involved and provide support without attachment to the situation, the other person, or your idea of how people should act and how life should be. When you show up in a clear and emotionally centered space, you are being the best support possible—you are mentally and emotionally available to assist from a state of love without your ego's vested and jaded interest running the show.

Stop *Shoulding* on Yourself

It will take effort to be involved in an unattached manner. You'll likely feel strong resistance from the ego to actively support a person that doesn't conform to your ideals or shoulds. The ego will want to offload the heavy energy of your shoulds and find release through blowing up at others, criticizing them for not doing as they should, or giving them the silent treatment. These externalized actions may feel better in the body initially as the heavy energy dissipates relatively quickly and painlessly, but it's not functional because it only exacerbates the problem and hurts the other and ourselves through repeated problems and dis-ease in our bodies and lives.

When we start *shoulding* on ourselves, the only thing we create is strife and struggle—for ourselves and others. When you hear yourself (either internally or externally) say "should," be mindful and question whether this is a fact and natural law in the world. Or perhaps it's a thought to which you're clinging that isn't serving you or the other and can be traded in for a higher thought that will create more harmony in your situation.

Another way to view unattachment to our shoulds is to let go. Again, I'm not saying don't give a crap. What you're letting go of is your *thoughts* about the way things should be. When we let go, we accept the way something *is*, despite our displeasure with it. As we covered in forgiveness, accepting or acknowledging does not mean that we agree with what has happened (or is happening), we simply see something as it is.

See and acknowledge what is as it is and release the shoulds.

Life will be more fun.

Let Go and Let God

Our ego minds create a feeling of safety by conforming to the known, and it's our past knowns that make up our shoulds. When something foreign arises, we try to control it and things outside of ourselves to conform to our shoulds so we can feel safe and comfortable. This is the primary reason people struggle with change: it leads to scared feelings of the unknown. There is no point of reference, and the ego freaks out.

Kids should go to school, graduate, and get a job to be happy and successful. That's what I knew based on what I was taught. And before I started mastering my inner world, I over-reacted when Zeydan's report card grades were low. My mind fretted over the what-ifs; I mean, I had always scored eighty or more in school. What would this mean for Zeydan's future? I lashed out at him to get him to conform to what was normal in my mind. But it was useless and did more harm than good. Holding on to my beliefs and shoulds created great strife, both internally with my emotions and externally with my relationship with my son.

But as I did my work, I began to see things at face value. I began to see Zeydan as his own person who was doing his best. I stopped trying to control his behaviour to get him to conform to the ideals I had about him and how his life and our mother-son relationship should be. I let go of my knowns and became comfortable with the unknown. I made everything okay in my mind.

Would I have liked and wished my son's situation to be different?

Absolutely.

Do I wish that I had the close and tender relationship today that we had when he was younger?

Absolutely.

But I trust that God has a greater plan. He's got the box with the picture of the whole puzzle—my analytical mind does not. Let go and trust that life (God) knows what it's doing!

Letting go of our attachments and our shoulds doesn't mean we don't do everything in our power to try to get things to be different and what we feel is best according to our limited perceptions. But when our efforts to help and intervene are continually met with resistance, and they cause more harm than help, it may be time to approach the situation from a different perspective.

No one wants to get abused, divorced, lose a job, be ill, or experience anything that doesn't feel good, but sometimes these harsh and painful events provide us with precisely what is needed to grow and move into grander circumstances in life. It takes considerable work and effort for the butterfly to emerge from its cozy cocoon. Without the great exertion, the wings don't entirely develop, and the half-formed butterfly withers and dies. Only through painful birthing and breaking through its old shell is it possible for the butterfly to take flight and soar.

The emerging butterfly may put forth great effort, but it doesn't struggle. It instinctively goes through the necessary process and works at it. Struggle is effort laced with denial and resistance. Struggle results when we don't accept something as it is and instead wish it were another way. It's when we're chained to our mental constructs of how something should be. We stay out of the present moment, out of happiness, and stuck in despair.

With what are you struggling in your own life? To what beliefs or ideals are you holding that are not serving you or the other?

It takes conscious effort and vigilance to observe and let go of our minds' attachments. We need developed breathing skills to get to a place where we can override our mind's reactivity and tendency to cling to outdated thoughts and shoulds and instead observe, accept, and support through unattached involvement.

It's only through using these tools that I can have fun and experience unconditional happiness every day (yes, *every* day) in a life that looks entirely opposite to the happily ever after that I had dreamed of and desperately chased my entire life.

When in Doubt, Laugh

If we've healed from a past traumatic event, and time has since elapsed, we often look back, reminisce, tell stories, and chuckle about the whole thing. If we can laugh about something after it has passed, why can we not get to that point sooner and laugh about it now?

We look back on the banes of our lives and realize that, in fact, they were blessings. Yet, as we're going through situations in real-time, we lose sight of this and the understanding that things are happening *for* us. We judge what we are going through as bad because it doesn't conform with our ideals or shoulds, and we stress about it.

But feeling distraught and stressed will not assist anyone; in fact, it will exacerbate the heaviness. During a time of struggle, remind yourself that, *although this may be tough, and it hurts like heck, I will look back on this as a blessing.*

Breathe and remember that life is happening *for* you. Watch your emotions rise and work with them—they are your signposts and gifts on your journey to self-mastery. Enjoy the fact that you can witness this crazy movie unfolding. Be amused by it. Heck, might as well get some popcorn, flash a smile, give a chuckle, and enjoy the movie.

Having fun and laughing not only helps ease our mind-made stress in situations, but it is also healing. Science has proven that laughter changes our body chemistry and raises our energy levels—the use of therapy dogs leverages this known phenomenon.

Why *not* laugh and have fun?

What is stopping you?

Hint: look inside, not out!

By intentionally choosing to have fun and laugh, the only thing you stand to lose is your attachment to the ideas of the way things should be and your attachment to the idea that you need to suffer and stress out.

Once again, your ego may very well question and reject this idea. Just assure that needy ego that it's reasonable to react like that but that you're going to handle this one with your eyes wide open and choose to create levity and feel at ease with what is before you.

Talk to your ego, tell it *Aha! I see what's happening here. And it's normal for you to want to react like that. But I'm on to you. And we're going to get through this in a reasonable manner that feels good. I get to choose how I feel—not YOU, ego. Go sit in the backseat.*

And then laugh at the fact that you could be classified as insane because you're talking to an aspect of yourself as though it were another person in your head. Rest assured, it's all You, and it's all good.

With knowledge of the principles outlined in this book, trusting in the creative flow of life, and applying your LIFE Method™ with patience and persistence, you'll be able to transmute fretting into fun and enjoy every day, regardless of what it brings.

Let all of it be good. Let it be fun.

CHAPTER 8

Evolve: It's Why You're Here

The more you know yourself, the more you know God.

—*Orest Bedrij*

Evolution is always happening, with or without our intention and intervention. It's as natural as the birth and death of the body, the rise and fall of the sun, and the ebb and flow of the tide.

But here's the thing. Are you going to evolve consciously or unconsciously?

To evolve consciously, we need to live with one eye always looking on the inside knowing that our worlds mirror the energy of who we are. And if we don't like what we're experiencing on the outside, be it career, relationships, health, or finances, we work with the energy on the inside. We regularly check in with our inner sight and internal terrain, because this is where the real work, the work that truly impacts our lives, happens.

As we move through our lives with conscious awareness and commitment to doing our inner work, we consciously evolve into higher versions of ourselves. We change our energy, and our outer worlds and experiences change as a natural consequence. When we choose conscious evolution, we become intentional creators of our lives, that soon fill with grace, ease, and unconditional happiness—the way life was intended.

Sign me up, right?

Like the butterfly exerts immense effort to emerge from its cocoon, so too must we exert effort to shift from our old limiting views and ways of being into new and empowering ones. In addition to the practices already covered, the following tools will help to further your ascent in becoming the conscious creator of your life and to experience your unconditionally happy now.

Breathe and Meditate

Yes. Again.

I'm sounding like a broken record intentionally. I want to stress how vital our breath is to our health and wellbeing. If there's one practice you take away from this book, it's to breathe deeply, mindfully, and often.

When we inhale into the lower lobes of our lungs, cellular oxygen uptake increases, and an aerobic environment is created. In the presence of oxygen, our cells thrive and are effectively able to thwart invaders and diseases that fester in anaerobic conditions. As a regular practice, deep breathing will give you the greatest reward for the effort you put in. As an emergency practice in challenging situations, deep breathing will help calm the reactive mind and put your body into a state of ease rather than fight-or-flight.

The second part of our breathwork is awareness, because deep breathing will only do so much if our minds are scampering about with an array of fear-based thoughts and what-if scenarios. These types of thoughts generate stress hormones, that essentially negate the wonderful oxygenated environment that was created through deep breathing. Focus your mind on the breath during both your regular meditation practice as well as during those challenging moments. Keep that mind fixed upon what really matters: not the story outside, but the one that's inside. And as you bring the mind and the breath home inside yourself, a sense of peace and calm will result, and the outside world will reflect this for you.

At a minimum, include five minutes of quiet, mindful breathing practice, every day. I think you've got ten minutes in you, though. Ideally, it's twenty.

Choose Your Thoughts, Feelings, and Words

In Chapter Six, we learned that our thoughts create beliefs, our beliefs affect our actions, repeated actions form habits, and that we become the collective of our habits which creates our personality and experience of life. Without question, our thoughts (known or unknown) about ourselves, others, and life shape our perceptions and our worlds. So, to change your world and your experiences, simply change your thoughts, right?

The trick is to be aware of your thoughts, and the tools presented in this book will help you to cultivate the needed skill of mindful awareness. The moment something unwelcomed appears in your life, get fully present and listen to the thoughts your mind begins to spout, because the thoughts that erupt under stress will shed light on your subconscious limiting beliefs that would otherwise be transparent to you.

Keep in mind that our egos will place a spin on observed information to categorize it and make it meaningful within the context of our belief systems and our past experiences: that's a polite way to say that our egos judge.

Consider a rainy day. We may say "it's miserable outside" because that's what we believe based on our past experiences and what we learned from our parents and from everyone else that told us so. Now consider that in some countries, rain is a sacred element that is believed to pour blessings onto those it touches. Those people welcome rain with joy and declare that "It's beautiful outside."

Who's right?

Who's happier?

The only thing preventing you from being happy in the rain of your life is your thoughts about it. As soon as you label something as bad, you unknowingly condition your experience to conform to that label.

Why not choose thoughts and labels that will create a positive and happy experience? After all, that which appears bad, like a ruptured appendix or an auto collision, is often good because it's precisely what is needed for personal awakening and growth and to make permanent changes for the better—it just may not feel good in the body at the moment.

Labelling something or someone or their behaviour as bad creates struggle and strife for all involved. Maintaining objective thoughts about ourselves and others is a means to choose higher thoughts and avoid limiting judgments. Stick to commenting on observable facts and natural laws, and you'll open yourself to experiencing higher vibrations that feel good.

Sounds simple enough, right?

Be aware, it may not be easy to remain on a judgment-free diet with consistency because of the decades of engrained subconscious judgments and labels that have been programmed in your mind and applied to your days. Remember, veering from well-worn paths takes effort! Not to mention, that the silver lining to the seemingly bad situation or experience may not be apparent immediately and may take weeks, months, and, yes, perhaps years, to realize the benefit of that which has transpired. It takes faith and trust in the perfection of life.

Having said that, when (not if, but when), your mouth spits off a limiting label about yourself, your abilities, or something or someone, simply "take it back"—just like you did when you were a kid and you heard someone say something mean. It works. Simply say "I cancel that," or "I take that back," or "I didn't mean that... what I actually meant to say was..." and replace the limiting judgment with a neutral and factual statement. In the case of a rainy day you could say "it's raining outside," or better yet, "I bet that grass is loving this rain. I'm so grateful that we have an abundance of clean water in this country."

Just as we can select thoughts that are based on observable and tangible information, so too can we choose thoughts that are based in love rather than fear. When we train our minds to take the backseat and allow our Higher Selves to drive, we can consciously choose to think, speak, and act in ways that align with the energy of love. When we do this, our growth is exponential and everyone involved benefits immensely. The energy of love is the highest vibration that we can experience. Love transmutes all. Choose love when the protective ego would rather blame, criticize, and defend. Then watch conflict dissolve.

We can apply a similar practice and create a lighter feeling in our bodies when our emotions are frantic and running the show. As soon as we can recognize that the mind and emotions are getting worked up and sucked into drama, we can come back to the senses in the body—see, feel, hear, smell and listen to your surroundings, and then ask yourself: "Am I okay right now?"

Chances are you have food in your belly, a warm shelter in which you're sitting or standing, clothes on your body, and maybe even a car in the driveway. The only problem that exists is the mind rehashing the past (which it can't change) or fretting about the future (which hasn't happened yet and which it can't control). Settle the rampant, unproductive, and sabotaging thoughts by focusing the mind on the present—here and now—and use your physical senses to help you achieve this.

Then, rinse and repeat.

And sprinkle with a dash of generating the feeling of love in the body.

~⚯~

> **Your outer experience reflects your inner thoughts that you have chosen to hold.**

Before we leave this important topic of thoughts, feelings, and words, I want to stress how powerful these are! Each of these aspects of ourselves creates our reality. Everything in existence started with a thought. Thoughts are things, we just can't see them. We don't see electricity either, but we believe in it because of its effects. Likewise, every thought you think has an effect, you just can't see it immediately. Your outer experience reflects your inner thoughts that you have chosen to hold. If you repeatedly think the same thought, you will eventually see the physical effects of it.

Words and actions are the first steps for thoughts to manifest into the physical—they pack a little more oomph than thoughts alone.

When a pebble is dropped into a bowl of water, what happens to the ripples when they reach the edge? They don't just stop, right? They return to the source from which they came.

My friend, the source is *you*, and the ripples are your thoughts, words, feelings, and actions. This is the premise behind karma (you reap what you sow).

Be impeccable and precise with your thoughts, words, and actions. Guard each with utmost care, attention, and intention. Think and speak the highest good of yourself, others, and conditions. If you can't say something that isn't uplifting, don't say it. And if you happen to think it or speak it and manage to catch yourself doing so, then take it back. Let each thought and word matter and have a positive impact in the world. Send ripples that will serve you and others—yes, even the people that piss you off; after all, what do you stand to lose by blessing your enemy, other than your ego's pride?

There are two powerful practices I'd like to leave you with on this matter. The first is "I AM". These two words represent creation. It is how our Higher Selves came to be as an individualized aspect of God. As part of Creation itself, our Higher Selves are nothing short of the same perfection as our Creator. Anything that you think or utter after "I AM" should reflect this divine perfection.

I know. That's a big leap.

How about we just start with placing a positive spin on every word that follows "I AM"? You will come to create and experience the thoughts and words that follow that powerful duo. For example, when asked how you are doing, instead of responding with "I'm tired," try saying "I'm feeling a little better now, thanks for asking."

You'll figure it out.

Have fun with it.

It's a big one though. Almost as big as mindful deep breathing!

To help remind you of your rightful inheritance and qualities you can express after stating 'I AM," a Table of Divine Qualities is provided for you at the back of this book.

Secondly, when our thoughts and words are coupled with strong feelings, it sets the wheels of creation into motion. That which you think or say backed with strong feelings (whether heavy or light), will be turbo-boosted into manifestation. Remember this when you're upset and angry! Be impeccable with your words, especially when your ego is triggered—shut your mouth and walk away.

Use this phenomenon to help manifest your goals sooner. When you desire something, generate a feeling of love, excitement, or gratitude and hold the thought of that which you desire in your internal vision for at least fifteen seconds. See it as though it's already come to pass. Give thanks for it in advance.

The amount of inner work you've done and self-mastery you've achieved will determine the speed with which your thoughts manifest into physical reality. You need to clear the weeds and water the garden to promote the growth of the seeds that you've planted.

> **The thoughts you think today will shape the person you become tomorrow.**

Your old thoughts shaped you to become the person you are today, and the thoughts you think today will shape the person you become tomorrow. Choose to think thoughts that are rooted in love and are greater than your habitual thoughts and reactive emotions. This is where gratitude comes in handy.

Be Grateful

When you pause and feel grateful for something or somebody, your energy instantly shifts. You cannot be in a state of gratitude and feel a heavy emotion at the same time. It's impossible because the feeling of appreciation and that of a lower emotion are vibrating at two different frequencies, and the higher resonance always wins. When you open the door to a darkened room, the light seeps into the darkness, the darkness doesn't dampen the light, right? It's a natural law.

When you notice that you're caught up in the drama of life and your mind and emotions are taking you for a ride, run through these simple steps of gratitude:

1. Start with your deep belly breathing.

2. Recall a person or thing for which you're thankful.

3. Visualize the fine details of the person or thing.

4. Come up with at least three reasons *why* you're grateful for them.

5. *Feel* love and appreciation in your body. Let that feeling expand through you.

6. Repeat with at least two additional people/things for which you're grateful.

Several years ago, I watched Oprah Winfrey on *Super Soul Sunday* as she spoke of her gratitude journal, and ever since I've been practicing gratitude, whether it's through a journal or my thoughts, feelings, and words. When my kids were younger, I had them write three things to be grateful for each night before bed. Although they eventually came to hate the activity because I was attached to the idea and became like a bootcamp instructor who forced them to do it. But I digress.

Filling your mind with gratitude and changing your emotional state to one of reverence and appreciation is immensely beneficial, especially before you doze off at night. When you sleep, your body enters a state of rest and repair, and when your body is filled with the elevated energy of gratitude, the restoration of your cells gets a turbo-boost.

Likewise, beginning your days with gratitude sets the stage for the entire day. Before stepping out of bed in the morning (especially before reaching for your mobile device), reflect on the things for which you're grateful using the steps outlined above. This could be as simple as being thankful for the warm sheets in which you're snuggled, the secure roof over your head, or the fact that you're alive and breathing and experiencing another day as you. Place a sticky note on your phone as a reminder to practice this new and powerful habit before you begin your day in a reactive mode by looking at your phone.

Whether morning or night, and whether written, spoken, or imagined, the essential component to your practice of gratitude is to allow the energy of appreciation to resonate in your body—to *feel* grateful. Since feelings have a physical vibration to them, the energy in your body begins to shift and nudges the cells in your body to change and align with it. The magic and healing powers of gratitude alter the cellular environment—you change your energy. And you attract what you are (your energy), not what you want.

Allow

It's easier to swim in a river going with the current rather than against it, right?

The same is true in life. The universe has a rhythm and a pulse—a natural intelligent movement or flow of energy. This universal flow is all-present, all-knowing, and all-powerful, and when left to do its thing, the seemingly miraculous happens: babies are born into the world, the sun rises every morning, wounds heal and new skin grows.

Our Higher Selves are one with this universal intelligence and flow, and when we connect with our Higher Selves, we connect with this flow. When we fight, resist, or try to control *what is* and go against the current, struggle results. By *what is*, I'm referring to the things outside of ourselves over which we have no rightful control. The only things we have true control over are our own thoughts, feelings, words, and actions.

Shortly after I split from Seth, I went on a date with a guy for a group dance lesson. Being one who followed instructions with precision, I knew I'd be good at dancing. And the lesson was fantastic. I rocked! Then we partnered up for the social dance that followed. I sucked. I was frustrated as heck. I simply could not give up control. I wanted to lead, and having two leads in a partner dance is a recipe for trampled toes.

Almost eight years later, after intense life coaching studies and extensive inner personal work, I'm ecstatic to say that I'm now tearing up the dance floor (at least in my mind and body I think and feel like I am). The point is, I've learned to settle my ego's tendency to want to control everything. I trust in the flow of life and my dance partner, and the result is enjoyment, beauty, and harmony.

With everyday miracles like gravity, seasons, and blooming flowers, how could any "wrong" exist on this planet? We are situated on a gigantic sphere that is spinning at a thousand miles per hour while suspended in space. In fact, we're probably upside down right now. If something was not meant to be, it would not be. In this, trust that all things, even the seemingly terrible, are perfect and needed for the conscious evolution of all involved. Seeds must be sown into the darkness before they can sprout and thrive—similarly, situations that we perceive as harsh are often essential to provide the ideal growth conditions to enter a new phase. It's like a period of incubation.

> **Replace the need to control with the confidence of conviction.**

With this perspective in mind, letting go of our small ideas of how we think something or someone should be, becomes a little easier. Replace the need to control with the confidence of conviction that something more significant is going on than your physical senses and mind are telling you.

With the deep love and care that I have for Zeydan and the wonderful memories we shared as he was growing up, never could I have imagined that I wouldn't be an actively involved mother in his life. Never could I have dreamt that he would be in the circumstances that he is in. But this is where things currently are. It has become what it is, and I am there every step of the way to support Zeydan, regardless of what that support may look like.

I trust in the perfection of life and the grand picture, even and especially when it comes to one of the most intimate bonds in life—that between a mother and her child. There's more going on here than my limited mind can see. I have faith and trust that all is well and is as it is intended to be. And it's through my consistent inner work that I can be a strong and unconditionally loving support for Zeydan.

When your mind would like to judge a situation as bad, refrain from doing so.

1. Trust in the divine flow and perfection of life while simultaneously taking action and applying unattached involvement where possible. If something was not meant to be, it would not be.

2. Do your deep breathing exercises, practice gratitude, and send a blessing.

3. Trust that banes become blessings and affirm that God's wisdom and greater intelligence is transpiring before you.

4. Silently affirm, *Thy Will (not my will) be done.*

You'll keep your energy elevated and will be at your greatest for those whose lives you touch. Allowing anything less than this will not help the situation, but your elevated energy and blessings will.

Move

As Energy Beings, we are at our best when our energy is flowing, and our mindful breathing practices promote this fluidity. Another more obvious way to get energy moving in our bodies is quite simply to move!

The numerous benefits of exercise are well-known: it brings oxygen and life into the cells of our bodies. But the benefits go beyond our physiology. When we exert ourselves to the point where we must focus on catching our breath or endure physical discomfort during strenuous activity, then our minds join in to assist, and our movement becomes like a meditation.

When you physically exert yourself, you bring your mind into your body—where it belongs! And when you're focused internally, it also means your mind isn't running rampant with wasteful negative thinking.

If you're not engaging in physical activity regularly, take inventory of how you spend your time during your days. Are there moments when you could include fifteen minutes of physical activity in place of sedentary activity? Or are there routine activities during which you could include movement, like taking the stairs, parking farther from the door, or doing squats, push-ups, and lunges while watching television? The possibilities are only limited by how willing you are to act rather than make excuses.

Yoga, when practiced as it was initially intended, brings awareness into parts of our bodies that are unknown to us. Just like an emotional trigger will bring our awareness to a part of us begging for our attention, yoga will bring our attention to restricted places in our body. Yoga and our practice of allowing go together: as we learn to let go and stop resisting *what is*, we grow more fully into ourselves. With flexibility in our minds and lives comes flexibility in our bodies, and vice versa. The result is resilience, fluidity, and agility—physically, mentally, emotionally, and spiritually.

Get curious about the spaces in your body that are tight and restricted. Breathe loving awareness into those spaces. Become and stay active. Start moving. Do yoga.

Connect with Life

The closer we get to nature and the natural flow of life, the more aligned we become with our Higher Selves, and the more gracious and enjoyable our lives become.

Where best to connect with nature than in nature?

Your dwelling may dictate the feasibility of this practice, but where possible and as often as possible, immerse yourself in nature. Notice the trees and how they simply accept and allow. Regardless of external conditions, trees continue to be trees and weather the storms. Their deeply buried roots (your connection to God and your Higher Self) enable them to stand tall and resilient, while their trunks (your body) provide the means to channel nutrients and energy, and the branches (your thoughts, words, and deeds) engage in the outer world.

Trees remain still, silent, and stable, and they continue to serve life through their beauty and their endless supply of oxygen and shelter. We have a lot to learn from trees, and when we get still and quiet in their presence, we connect with their energy and the universal flow of nature and life. When we do this mindfully, our physiology and energy shift—we attune ourselves to nature.

We can further attune ourselves to nature by eating foods that are as close to nature as possible. The fewer hands and mechanical or chemical processes that have touched our food, the greater the purity and energy that will be available to infuse into our cells as we digest it. Foods from the earth that are raw and untreated provide us with the greatest connection to life compared to those that have been processed, bagged, boxed, or canned. These fresh and unaltered foods create an alkaline environment for our cells, which, like oxygen, promotes optimal conditions for our cells to flourish, recuperate, and regenerate. If you're reading between the lines, this means eat lots of organic and raw fruits and vegetables. If this is new for you, start small and let your body adjust as you introduce new foods.

What Now?

Practice makes permanent. I'd say practice makes perfect, but we are already perfect exactly as we are.

Wait. What?

Yes, paradoxically, we're both. We are perfect, and at the same time we are continually growing and consciously evolving to become greater versions of ourselves.

It took me a while to fully grasp that one.

It is only through repeated use and practice of your LIFE tools that they will become part of your subconscious and a way of being. It will take steadfast commitment and patience to persevere in your application of these tools because the conditioned and deeply embedded beliefs and patterns developed through the decades will be your default route. And the mind would rather go with the ease and comfort of the known rather than the work and discomfort of the unknown. The unknown scares the heck out of the ego because it can't control what it doesn't know. So be prepared to reassure the hesitant and frightened part of you that will resist doing your inner work and implementing these practices.

Be patient with your efforts and your progress and refrain from judging them. Trust that each action you take to apply a practice is one step closer to becoming the master and conscious creator of your life.

While applying these tools to create new habits, intentionally change your old ones. I mean this in a light and simple way. If you go through the same motions getting ready in the morning and getting into bed at night, switch it up. Sleep on the opposite side of the bed (gasp), brush your teeth with the opposite hand, drive a different route to work, or put on your clothes in a different sequence. You get the idea. Just keep it fun! Through doing these small changes, the neurological network in your brain expands and the protective ego gets accustomed to small unfamiliar changes.

The result?

Your ego will come to trust that new things are safe, and it'll be easier for you to implement bigger changes. This is kind of a big deal!

When you commit to doing the practice of your inner work with persistence, patience, and perseverance, expect your life to change, just like it did for one of my students. When Chrystal started her inward journey, she was unhappy and drowning in her emotions. Having been controlled by her mother growing up and then her husband for decades after, Chrystal knew only how to be an obedient daughter, a committed and loving mother, and a controlled and disciplined wife. She wasn't allowed to work so she cared for her four children full-time. She developed a deep and loving bond with each of her children; they meant the world to her.

But as young teens, the children were brutally alienated and completely estranged from Chrystal by her husband while they went through their divorce. She didn't have the confidence or personal power to stand up for herself and make a change. She felt victimized, betrayed, and deeply saddened for the loss of her children. Emotional anguish contaminated almost every waking moment of Chrystal's days—she felt lost. She felt that her life had no meaning without her children.

Today, Chrystal's young adult children are still not actively involved in her life, but after only twenty weeks of coaching and her dedicated and persistent inner investigation and work, Chrystal identified and released her limiting subconscious beliefs and reprogrammed empowering ones. She gained her voice, confidence, and a sense of self-worth and self-love. She now realizes that she is her own person—one with power and permission to be herself, which she has learned is so much more than being only a daughter, a mother, and a wife.

Through her inner work, Chrystal realized that she can't control her children's or ex-husband's words or actions to conform with her desires to make her feel better. She gained control of her thoughts and chose to think greater and feel higher. She accepts *what is* and is happy despite her life not looking the way to which she had been formerly attached. When her vengeful ex-husband and bewildered and begrudged children present challenging situations, Chrystal uses her tools and remains mentally and emotionally grounded and responds to her ex-husband with confidence and to her estranged children with compassion and unconditional love.

Chrystal's life is just one of many lives that have transformed, as has mine, through consistent use of the LIFE Method™.

Commit to your practices and connect with like-minded souls who are embarking on their individual paths of conscious evolution. Together, we stand stronger. Together, regardless of physical distance, we harmonize, synchronize, and synergize our energy. Where two or more gather in the name of personal growth and learning, each member is carried further together than they would from working alone.

Sharing our struggles and successes with kindred souls on similar inward journeys brings a sense of ease and okayness, especially when we're having a rough go at it. Supporting one another through our difficulties and celebrating our wins is one of the greatest gifts we can give to ourselves and one another. For this purpose, I've created a free online community for beautiful souls, just like you, that will synergize your personal growth and conscious evolution.

As you do your inner work, your energy begins to align with the vibration of your Higher Self, and you begin to remember who you truly are. You start sensing your subtle intuition (communications from your Higher Self) and you follow it with increasing faith. Things get interesting, and all sorts of so-called coincidences and synchronicities start happening—the perfect people appear in perfect timing. Soon you come to expect the so-called miracles.

You embrace fear and get curious about it. You start making different, unfamiliar decisions, and each new choice is a step toward the greatest version of yourself and your self-mastery.

You become empowered and amazingly resilient and you embrace challenges with ease, although the appearance of such challenges significantly diminishes. You begin to sense tense situations before they arise, and you head them off at the pass. The struggle that was once necessary for you to awaken is no longer needed. You shift from being the observer of your life to the conscious creator of it. You experience and admire all sorts of amazing and beautiful things that your mind formerly would have overlooked or judged.

You're happier more often and love starts to be your predominant feeling. People think you're slightly crazy because you're happy for no apparent reason, and you simply revel in the fact that you don't even care because how you feel about yourself does not depend on the opinions of others. You're steadfast and confident in the Truth of who you are. And you are madly in love with yourself and life.

Dear Friend, these LIFE Method™ practices are free and accessible anytime and anywhere. They need only *you* and your emotional willingness and dedication to apply them in your project of LIFE.

Make your life the paved downhill road lined with lemonade stands on a balmy summer's day.

Get to know and come to trust this Inner Presence… your Higher Self. With it comes a state of tranquility and love that is faithfully there for you. In fact, it *is* You.

Day in and day out, you feel an abundance of joy, vitality, and love. And bonus: physical ailments resolve as a by-product of your elevated energy and purer state of being.

You won't need a reason to be happy. It'll be your default state.

You'll no longer wait for it to happen.

You'll just be.

Happy.

Table of Divine Qualities

Below is a list of inherited qualities that you have rightful access to claim in this very moment.

To help realize your divine aspects, declare them through *I AM* statements with power, purpose, passion, and praise!

Repeat often.

Remember: You are perfect exactly as you are!

I AM...

Supportive	Powerful	Beauty	Forgiveness
Abundance	Fluidity	Committed	Stillness
Confidence	Grace	Truth	Dedication
Self-reliance	Fearlessness	Generous	Courageous
Faith	Discernment	Healing	Prudence
Open	Light	Vigilance	Gentleness
Tranquility	Humility	Health	Innocence
Magnificence	Joy	Love	Benevolence
Harmony	Patience	Mercifulness	Meticulousness
Understanding	Free	Omnipotence	Omniscience
Trustworthiness	Righteousness	Peace	Perfection
Oneness	Diligence	Purity	Responsible
Compassionate	Awareness	Sacredness	Authentic

Acknowledgments

Oh my goodness. I could make this section into a book on its own. Without each of these players in my Project: LIFE, I wouldn't be who, what, or where I am today. Every person, every event and every thing, no matter how seemingly insignificant, plays an intricate role in our lives.

To *My Dear Readers*: Thank you for affording me the most valued gifts we can give to another—your presence, time, and attention. Thank you for embarking on your journey and being curious enough to pick up and explore this book. Trust in your project of LIFE. Trust that it's all good, even the seemingly bad stuff. You are powerful beyond your mind's imagination and can experience happiness in this moment and create the life you truly desire. I love you.

To *My Beloved Children:* You have been my greatest teachers. Thank you for putting up with my foibles and attempts at learning while I was excavating my Gem. I am so proud of you both, and I am blessed, delighted, and honoured to be your mother. Keep shining your light and doing you. I love you, eternally.

To *My Mom and Sister:* You've been by my side every step of my journey and it is through your strength, unconditional love, and support that I am who I am today. Mom, you are the strongest woman I know. Thank you for enduring your tumultuous past "for the kids" while still managing to love me as fiercely as you did. Know that it was not in vain. The degree of fear you overcame to finally end the abuse in your life is admirable, and I'm so proud of you.

To *My StepStepDad:* Thank you for being Mom's knight in shining armour and for being true to your heart and encouraging Mom to do the same. I can't imagine what life would have been like without your presence. I am eternally grateful for your big heart and courage.

To *Roger:* You were my anchor during the toughest time of my life. Your endless giving and ability to laugh are priceless. Without you, I wouldn't be where I am today—thank you. You are so dear to me.

To *My Past Aggressors:* Without you, I wouldn't have unearthed and realized so many divine aspects of my Higher Self. I also wouldn't have a moving and powerful message to guide and inspire others and help contribute to the shift in consciousness of humanity. Thank you for doing your part in my great grand Project: LIFE… just like I requested.

To *My Dear Friends who have held my hand along the way:* Camaraderie is a powerful force and an essential gift in our project of LIFE. Thank you for your companionship, support, laughter, and love.

To *My Trusted Naturopathic Doctor:* Thank you for always being there for me and sharing your wisdom, support, and love.

To *The One Who Ignited the Spark in My Heart, Orest:* Your fervent dedication to cracking the code of existence and your devotion to sharing it with those of us who are in earnest readiness, turbo-boosted my ascent on my path. I'm so blessed to be led by your wisdom and love.

To *My Spiritual Mentor, George:* Your purity, wisdom, and divine guidance led me to the Light path and kept me on it, especially during the toughest time of my life. Through your commitment in helping others step into their divine abilities, I now know how to transcend and transmute discord and come home to the Truth of Light, Love, and Perfection. I am so blessed and eternally grateful for your Presence and gracious support.

To *My Spiritual Life Coach and Teacher at Holistic Learning Centers, Hu Dalconzo*: Without your steadfast loyalty to your path, I would not be who or where I am today. Through your powerful and effective HuMethod™ and your guidance and support, you've made it possible for me to shed the subconscious crap that was dimming my Light, so I could hop on my dharmic path and help transform the lives of others. Thank you, thank you, thank you.

To *Dr. Sue Morter at Morter Institute:* Your brilliant and effective Energy Codes® training has provided me with concrete tools to transcend the stubborn energetic blocks which remained hidden from my consciousness. Through your steadfast dedication to sharing your knowledge and committing to your purpose and Truth, I am inspired and able to do the same. With deep love and reverence, thank you.

To *My Publisher and Book Coach at Author Academy Elite, Kary Oberbrunner and Team*: You are a true motivator and influencer and are changing the lives of many. Thank you for making this book possible through your experience, knowledge, and solid support system. You totally rock!

To *My Beta-readers—Annastasia, Beatriz, Cheryl, Darlene, Marcie, and Melissa; my Editor— Jody; and my Proofreaders— Inna and Kathy:* Thank you for your keen eyes and valuable insights to help shape my message into one that is clear, clean, and meaningful. Your love, support, and encouragement mean more than you know. I'm so blessed and grateful that your energy has been interwoven through these pages.

To *Cheeko, My Little Editor*: Everyone has something to learn from a dog. You're the best poochie ever.

To *God and His Legions of Light Workers*: Only feelings can express my reverence and gratitude for this experience of life and your eternal guidance.

To *My Back-Then, Present, and Future Self*: You did it, Girl! I'm so proud of you! Keep shining your Light and staying connected to You. We're just getting started. The best is yet to come!

Peace Be Still. All Is Well.

About the Author

Christine Grauer is an author, motivational speaker, and spiritual life coach on a fiery mission helping women who feel lost and defeated to transcend their past hurts and current circumstances. She helps empower women to break free from painful life patterns and shift their mindset and energy to cultivate inner wisdom, confidence, and power so they can live rooted in unconditional happiness and love.

Having lived her life as "Mousie" and enduring abusive relationships, Christine's own empowerment came after her wake-up call. Since stepping through fear, ending abuse, and empowering herself, Christine's purpose and mission have become crystal clear.

With a Master of Science degree in Human Biology and Nutritional Science and a post-graduate Certificate in Adult Learning, Christine has spent over twenty years in health sciences and adult education. And for over twenty years, she's been an avid student of spirituality and quantum science culminating with certifications as an Energy Codes® Facilitator and Spiritual Life Coach.

Christine is committed to guiding and empowering her students to become conscious creators of their lives and to simply be—happy. Christine lives in Waterloo, Ontario, Canada, where she's a single-mother to two teens enjoying her time as an avid reader, a hot-room yogi, a runner, a Bachata dancer, and a fervent student of life. She walks her talk and lives each day with joy, vitality, unconditional happiness, and love.

Connect with Christine at ChristineGrauer.com.

CONNECT

- Surround yourself with like-hearted people
- Be inspired
- Synergize your growth
- Have fun

Join the *Project LIFERS* Private Facebook Community

https://www.facebook.com/groups/ProjectLIFEBook/

ON SOCIAL MEDIA,
CHECK OUT CHRISTINE'S:

- Inspirational vignettes
- Practical life coaching tips
- Occasional dance video

FACEBOOK.COM/CHRISTINEG.CA   INSTAGRAM.COM/CHRISTINEG.CA

Christine Grauer
speaker · author · coach

DISCOVER

Take Your LIFE Method™ Assessment and discover:

- How your current practices are serving you
- Your next key practice in your project of LIFE
- Your individualized LIFE affirmations
- The next best step toward your LIFE mastery

YourLIFEMethod.com

TRANSFORM

Through personal coaching with Christine:

- Find clarity
- Leave the past behind
- Overhaul your mindset
- Instill empowering beliefs
- Stride with confidence into tomorrow

ChristineGrauer.com/Contact

EXPERIENCE

You've read the book.
Are you ready for the experience?
Join Christine live.
ChristineGrauer.com/Events

SHARE

**Bring Christine to your
organization to:**

- Motivate your audience and shift their **mindset**
- Equip people with **practical tools** of transformation
- Awaken inherent **creativity** and power
- Instill **knowledge** to cultivate inner happiness
- Inspire to create empowering habits and lasting **change**

ChristineGrauer.com/Speaking

SUPPORT

20% of proceeds from *Project: LIFE* support non-profit youth wellness initiatives at the Covenant House!

Covenant House

Covenant House is pleased to be the recipient of donations from sales of *Project: LIFE!*

Covenant House helps youth ignite their potential and reclaim their lives. As Canada's largest agency serving youth who are homeless, trafficked or at risk, we offer the widest range of 24-7 services to about 350 young people each day.

As a national leader, we educate and advocate for long-term change to improve the lives of vulnerable youth. This includes influencing public policy, leading awareness and prevention programs and continually building and sharing our knowledge. As a learning organization, we strive for excellence and programs with impact.

More than a place to stay, we provide life-changing care with unconditional love and respect. We meet youth's immediate needs and then we work together to achieve their future goals. We offer housing options, health and well-being support, training and skill development, and ongoing care once youth move into the community.

Thanks to our donors, who contribute almost 80 percent of our $33 million annual operating budget, we are able to deliver these comprehensive programs and services.

Since 1982, Covenant House has supported more than 95,000 young people.